Grief

Svend Brinkmann

———

Grief

The Price of Love

Translated by Tam McTurk

polity

© Svend Brinkmann and Klim Publishers
First published in Danish as *Det Sørgende Dyr*, © Klim Publishers, 2018
This English edition © Polity Press, 2020

Polity Press
65 Bridge Street
Cambridge CB2 1UR, UK

Polity Press
101 Station Landing
Suite 300
Medford, MA 02155, USA

ISBN-13: 978-1-5095-4123-2
ISBN-13: 978-1-5095-4124-9 (pb)

A catalogue record for this book is available from the British Library.

Library of Congress Cataloging-in-Publication Data

Names: Brinkmann, Svend, author. | McTurk, Tam, translator.
Title: Grief : the price of love / Svend Brinkmann ; translated by Tam McTurk.
Other titles: Sørgende dyr. English
Description: English edition. | Cambridge ; Medford, MA : Polity, 2020. | Translated from Danish. | Summary: "Brinkmann yet again offers a brilliant and illuminating account of one of the core components of human experience - grief "-- Provided by publisher.
Identifiers: LCCN 2019041174 (print) | LCCN 2019041175 (ebook) | ISBN 9781509541232 | ISBN 9781509541249 (pb) | ISBN 9781509541256 (epub)
Subjects: LCSH: Grief. | Bereavement--Psychological aspects.
Classification: LCC BF575.G7 B7367 2020 (print) | LCC BF575.G7 (ebook) | DDC 155.9/37--dc23
LC record available at https://lccn.loc.gov/2019041174
LC ebook record available at https://lccn.loc.gov/2019041175

Typeset in 11 on 14 pt Sabon by
Servis Filmsetting Ltd, Stockport, Cheshire
Printed and bound in Great Britain by TJ International Limited

The publisher has used its best endeavours to ensure that the URLs for external websites referred to in this book are correct and active at the time of going to press. However, the publisher has no responsibility for the websites and can make no guarantee that a site will remain live or that the content is or will remain appropriate.

Every effort has been made to trace all copyright holders, but if any have been overlooked the publisher will be pleased to include any necessary credits in any subsequent reprint or edition.

For further information on Polity, visit our website: politybooks.com

Contents

Preface

This is a book about grief. It is not a treatment manual, personal account or self-help reference work for moving on. There are enough of those out there already, reflecting the widespread public interest in the phenomenon and the advent of 'complicated grief' as a clinical diagnosis. Any number of people will willingly offer their help to those who have suffered the loss of a loved one. Once deemed personal and private, the preserve of bereaved individuals and groups, grief has become a matter for professionals, something to be treated with medicine and addressed by institutions. Since almost everybody encounters the phenomenon at some point or other, the potential market for diagnosis and treatment is huge. Nonetheless, the focus of this book is not on intervention, therapy or other forms of treatment. Instead, it explores the very essence of grief – its phenomenology. It seeks to analyse the fundamental nature of grief as a universal human condition, while recognising that it varies enormously depending on factors such as time and culture. The aim is to temper the debate about the medicalisation and pathologisation of grief, which is addressed in the final chapter.

The book has emerged from an ongoing research project, 'The Culture of Grief', which has been generously funded by the Obel Family Foundation. The project looks at how individuals experience grief, but also at collective mourning and how it relates to contemporary culture. Its many sub-projects – and indeed, this book – focus solely on the grief caused by bereavement. Although it is valid to discuss grief more broadly, as a response to divorce, illness, redundancy or other traumatic experiences, it would be beyond the scope of this book – partly because the new psychiatric diagnoses refer specifically to grief in response to death, but also because it is important not to blur the focus. The book does not look at specific types of grief, but approaches it as a generic phenomenon, something about which universal points can be made. It seeks to analyse the general features of the phenomenon and its impact on both individuals and society. The premise – that it is possible to approach grief as a generic phenomenon – is, of course, open to challenge. Some might deny any similarity between, for example, a parent losing a child and the death of a grandparent. By adopting a phenomenological approach – examining the phenomenon in terms of how it is experienced by humans – the book attempts to uncover the common features in grief's many manifestations. The ultimate success of that endeavour will depend not just on the analyses included here, but also on other scholars adopting a similar approach.

I would like to thank my friends at Klim for embracing the original idea of publishing a book about grief – especially Michael Nonboe and Camilla Rohde

Søndergaard, who have been a huge help with my scientific work for many years. I would also like to thank Louise Knight in particular for publishing the English version, and Tam McTurk for yet another masterful translation. I also owe a huge debt of gratitude to my colleagues from 'The Culture of Grief' project for discussing the themes covered in the book: Ester Holte Kofod, Ditte Winther-Lindqvist, Allan Køster, Brady Wagoner, Ignacio Brescó, Luca Tateo, Anne Suhr, Mikkel Krause Frantzen, Peter Clement Lund, Alfred Bordado Sköld and Anders Petersen – Ester, Allan and Anders in particular for their help in reviewing the manuscript. I am grateful to the whole team at Polity for all their help with the English version of the book. Finally, I would like to thank the Obel Family Foundation for so generously funding the five-year 'Culture of Grief' project, especially Britta Graae, with whom I enjoy an excellent working relationship in my capacity as head of research.

The theoretical ideas in this book were first explored in articles in the journals *Mortality* ('The body in grief'), *Culture & Psychology* ('Grief as an extended emotion', co-authored by Ester Holte Kofod), *Theory & Psychology* ('The grieving animal: Grief as a foundational emotion'), *Nordic Psychology* ('Could grief be a mental disorder?'), *Qualitative Inquiry* ('The presence of grief', co-authored by nine other scientists from 'The Culture of Grief') and *Integrative Psychological and Behavioral Science* ('General psychological implications of the human capacity for grief'). I would like to take this opportunity to thank the journal editors and peer reviewers for all of their work.

It is impossible to relate to grief purely analytically

– as a phenomenon to consider objectively, from a safe distance – because as adult human beings we have all, in one way or another, had personal experience of loss and grief. In February 2017, not long into 'The Culture of Grief' project, I lost my father. Ever since, I have had a peculiarly dualistic view of my own grief – both from the inside, by dint of the relationship between father and son, and from the outside, by virtue of my gradual accumulation of scientific, theoretical and empirical knowledge about the phenomenon. I have attempted to relate critically to the scientific theories through the lens of my personal experience, but I also believe that the research has helped me process my own loss. I would like to dedicate this book to the memory of my father, T.A. Christensen.

1

Introduction:
The Century of Grief

Grief has taken centre stage in how we reflect on life – not just in private, enclosed spaces, but also in public debate. The evidence is unavoidable. In the cultural sphere, interest in the phenomenon is reflected by the preponderance of grief-based memoirs and television documentaries. Musicians including Nick Cave, Arcade Fire, Mount Eerie, Leonard Cohen and David Bowie have all released albums and songs on the subject – the latter two almost literally sang their way to their graves. Bereavement discussion groups, cafés, operas and plays have emerged, and social media has created new spaces for sharing experiences of loss, grief and absence.

Michael Hviid Jacobsen, a sociologist specialising in death, has said that we live in 'the century of grief', which in his view began with the terrorist attacks of 11 September 2001.[1] Once a taboo subject, grief has entered the public sphere and collective consciousness, a trend that has coincided with a process of medicalisation that has situated grief in a healthcare context, culminating in the psychiatric diagnosis 'complicated grief'. The diagnosis seems set to reinforce the tendency to view grief as a medical and psychological matter, rather than an existential or religious one. At the same time, a range of organisations have also come to the fore that offer treatment to people whose parents, siblings or children are seriously ill or have died.

The century of grief is a 'post-secular' era, in which it is no longer widely believed that religion will peter out (McLennan 2010). We are witnessing a general revival of interest in religious, spiritual and existential questions – and grief, as a phenomenon, lies at the heart of these issues. The premise of this book is that grief is a basic existential phenomenon that occurs when love and death intersect. In order to experience the deep grief covered by this book, it is necessary to understand that a deceased loved one is irrevocably lost. Without love on the one hand, and an awareness of death's inevitability on the other, there is no genuine human grief. This brings us to the central thesis of this book: that humankind can be categorised as a grieving animal, because it appears to be a defining characteristic of our species that we are capable of relating profoundly and intimately to both love and death, which is a prerequisite for the ability to feel genuine grief. Other animals clearly feel separation anxiety and stress, and they too can have persistent, affective relationships with other beings that appear reminiscent of human love (think of the faithful dog). However, the book contends that it is only on the surface that other species appear to feel grief. Genuine grief is reserved for humankind, for better or worse. Worse, because grief hurts; better, because it is a meaningful pain, one that informs the entire network of emotional relationships that constitute the basic psychological substance of our lives. It is through grief that we maintain our bonds with the dead. Grief is – as is quite often and probably rightly said – the price we pay for love.

The philosopher Simon Critchley expresses a similar thought when he writes that the death of a loved one puts us in a position of 'radical impossibility' (2010: 40). It is an event over which we have no control. It is impossible to *will* the other's death away. There is nothing we can do. According to Critchley, the grief we feel invades and structures our subjectivity. He believes that humans can ultimately be categorised by our ability to grieve, and I concur (see especially Chapter 2). Grief tells us that we can never completely master life. We are forever doomed to fall short due to our dependency on others, who vanish from our lives. This may render us impotent, existentially speaking, but according to Critchley it is precisely this impotence, this fundamental fragility, that creates the ethical demand in our interactions with others. In that sense, grief and ethical life are interlinked.

This realisation – that grief is not just a simple pain to be cured, like a headache, but a meaningful experience following a loss – is reflected in popular culture. It is increasingly recognised that the goal is not to erase grief, to 'move on' and leave the dead behind, but to continue living with them. This is entirely consistent with recent grief theories, which emphasise continuing bonds (Klass, Silverman and Nickman 1996), whereas Freud, for example, believed that we should sever ties with the dead and reinvest our mental energy in new relationships (Freud 2005). New relationships can, of course, be significant and life-giving, but, thankfully, few would now argue that they should be at the expense of emotional bonds to the dead. If I may allow myself to

3

be normative here, at the beginning of the book, it is a central part of my thesis that we should incorporate the dead into our lives, not shut them out. But what does this mean in a day-to-day context?

Back to the things themselves

This book takes as its starting point the need to adopt a phenomenological approach in order to identify the nature of grief. Ever since Edmund Husserl, more than a century ago, phenomenology's watchword has been 'back to the things themselves!' In other words, the aim is to shed light on how people experience the world before forming scientific theories about it (for example, about grief as an illness or about its neurological basis). The book also contends that being able to describe grief's essential nature would help us to identify what is special about human beings, what distinguishes us from other living creatures. In this way, phenomenology is a philosophical and scientific (in this case, psychological) study of how a phenomenon manifests itself in our experience. The goal is to describe the essential structure of a phenomenon, also referred to as the *invariant* – in other words, that which remains constant throughout its manifestations.

At this point, it is worth pausing to outline the history of the phenomenological project that underpins this book. Phenomenology differs from the dominant theories in psychology, which seek to shed light on causal relationships and communicate them to the public. In a way, phenomenology goes back to ancient philosophy, including Aristotle (according to Nussbaum 1986), who believed that every study should start with an in-depth description of the phenomenon in question. *The description* of the phenomenon should precede any *explanation* of why it occurred and how it works. Aristotle argued that the scientific method had to be adapted to the phenomenon being studied, rather than the phenomenon being forced into pre-established scientific templates. Phenomena in mathematics require different methods than those in ethics.

The idea that the phenomenon takes precedence is an essential precondition for the phenomenological project. Husserl founded modern phenomenology around 1900. Martin Heidegger refined it as an existential philosophy, and Jean-Paul Sartre and Maurice Merleau-Ponty later steered it in an existential-dialectical direction (for more detail on the history of phenomenology see Brinkmann and Kvale 2015). The goal was to describe not only the phenomena in and of themselves, but in particular the underlying experience structures that make it possible for something to have its own special character. At first, under Husserl, phenomenology's primary focus was consciousness and life as it is experienced. This was later extended to encompass human experience as a whole, and Merleau-Ponty and Sartre also incorporated the body and human action in historical contexts into their thinking. Generally speaking, the goal of phenomenological research is to understand social and psychological phenomena from the actors' own perspectives, and to describe the world as experienced by individuals. Put simply, it is based on the assumption that what is important about reality is how people perceive it.

In psychology, it was Amedeo Giorgi in particular who, from the 1970s onwards, developed a phenomenological method for 'the study of the structure and the variations of structure of the consciousness to which any thing, event or person appears' (Giorgi 1975: 83). According to Merleau-Ponty (2012), it is a matter of describing the phenomenon in question as accurately and completely as possible, rather than seeking to explain or analyse it. This entails remaining faithful to the phenomenon studied in order to reach an understanding of its *essence* – the phenomenon's very being – by seeking out what is general about it. Husserl described one such method of doing so as 'free variation in the imagination'. In other words, the phenomenologist freely envisages all of the potential variant forms of a given phenomenon, and whatever is constant in the different iterations is its *being*. This involves a phenomenological *reduction*, i.e. disregarding general views about whether a given experience exists or not. The process can be described as 'putting in parentheses', as it consists of setting aside both general and theoretically advanced knowledge about the phenomenon in order to reach an unbiased description of its being (see Brinkmann and Kvale 2015: 49). It is worth quoting from Merleau-Ponty's programme for a phenomenology based on primary experiences of the world:

> Everything that I know about the world, even through science, I know from a perspective that is my own or from an experience of the world without which scientific symbols would be meaningless. The entire universe of science is constructed upon the lived world, and if we wish to think science rigorously, to appreciate precisely its sense and its scope, we must first awaken that experience of the world of which science is the second-order expression. (Merleau-Ponty 2012: p. lxxii)

Introduction: The Century of Grief

In geography, a map is an abstraction of the landscape in which we first directly encountered forests, towns and fields. Similarly, according to the phenomenological approach, scientific studies are abstractions based on immediate experiences in the world, to which we must find our way back in order to describe them. What does our emotional, psychological and social 'landscape' look like before we map it out in the form of scientific theories? Our experiences of grief, for example, precede our scientific and theoretical knowledge of it.

Since the days of Husserl, Heidegger, Sartre and Merleau-Ponty (all of whom I will refer to later in this book), phenomenology has branched out even further, to include even 'post-phenomenology', which not only looks at the experiential structures of the subjects involved, but also incorporates the meaning of the whole material and technological world. It might also be argued that Wittgenstein's philosophy of language, which has exerted a huge influence since the mid-twentieth century, is a kind of linguistic phenomenology that approaches philosophical questions by looking in detail at how language is used in certain contexts (Gier 1981). Wittgenstein is another starting point for this book – specifically, his contention that we can learn a great deal from scientific studies that describe the contexts in which we use linguistic concepts about emotions. Grief is not just a wordless state that we carry in our bodies, but a concept we learn to apply actively in certain situations. As such, gaining an awareness of how we acquire and use such concepts teaches us something important about the phenomenon. Viewed as an emotion, grief seems at once to be part of the human experience, an embodied state, an intersubjective form of communication and something deeply embedded in the social processes of culture. In my opinion, there is a need for a wide-ranging phenomenological approach to grief in order to understand both the depth and breadth of the phenomenon. This book presents a comprehensive proposal for such an approach.

Structure of the book

This introductory chapter concludes below with an outline of the history of grief. I then argue in Chapter 2 that grief is a phenomenon unique to human beings, as we have both a concept of death as the inevitable end point of life and the ability to love particular individuals. Love and death are both prerequisites for grief. Other species feel depressed and suffer separation anxiety, which superficially resembles grief, but I argue in this chapter that it is not actual grief – at least not in the way that humans grieve. Grief requires a reflexive awareness of finitude and emotional relationships that other species only possess on a rudimentary level. In this way, grief tells us something essential about human beings, that they can be understood as grieving animals, or at least as animals with the potential to grieve. If this is true, then humans should not just be understood as rational animals, as Aristotle believed (or *Homo sapiens*, the *thinking person*), but on a deeper level, as beings with the potential to have certain emotional relationships with the world and other people (we might call such a species *Homo sentimentalis*) – a potential that manifests itself, not least, in grief.

Chapter 3 follows up with a more focused phenomenological study of the *being* of grief. Based on Husserl's phenomenology – specifically as applied in Thomas Fuchs (2018) and Matthew Ratcliffe's studies of grief – it shows how grief manifests itself as the loss of a 'system of possibilities' (Ratcliffe 2017). In other words, the bereaved are left with a deep-rooted attachment to someone who has passed away. In poetic terms, it is a love that has become homeless. However, I also argue that this is where Husserl's phenomenology encounters its limits, as it risks reducing the experience of loss to nothing more than the bereaved's representations of the dead (a lost 'system of possibilities'). As a result, I supplement this position with Emmanuel Levinas's more radical phenomenology, which criticises the reduction of the deceased to their importance to the grieving self. According to Levinas, grief is not only about losing a 'system of possibilities', it is more fundamental – a loved one is no longer in this world. Grief has to be understood not only psychologically, but also ontologically.[2] This also explains why it is possible to grieve the loss of a loved one or of an idealised other to whom we may never have been close (e.g. idols or celebrities). The chapter also identifies some of the psychological implications of grief that challenge psychology's standard atomistic, functionalist (e.g. evolutionary psychology) and causal explanations. As an existential phenomenon, grief tells us something about humans as relational beings, and about psychology as a science that deals with a domain of reality that resists simple evolutionary or causal reduction.

Chapter 4 focuses specifically on grief as an embodied emotion. From ancient Greek tragedies to modern painting, the physical expression of grief has been

depicted in a fairly uniform manner. The chapter shows
how the experience of loss is recognised via the body of
the bereaved. Grief etches itself into us and we express
it physically. The basic thesis is that grief in some way
takes root in our physicality – the body itself is effectively in mourning. An analysis of the embodiment of
grief tells us something essential about human emotional life, and about the relationship between the mind,
the body and the world.

Chapter 5 examines grief as something that is not
only in the body but also in culture, in the form of material practices and systems of symbols. Grief is something
felt and enacted along with others in a cultural setting consisting of cemeteries, memorials, photo albums,
heirlooms and so forth. In other words, grief has both
socially and materially distributed aspects. Psychology is
plagued by a problematic individualism, in which grief
and other psychological phenomena are assumed to be
exclusively states that exist 'inside the mind' of the individual. Understanding grief as a socially and materially
distributed phenomenon bypasses this individualism. It
enables us to understand how grief is shared through
traditional cultural practices, and even 'outsourced'
to others, such as professional mourners, or 'keeners'
in Ireland. Music, rituals and physical objects help to
shape grief in a variety of ways. The chapter therefore
looks at the socio-material context of the experience of
loss and grief.

As a psychological phenomenon, grief is almost
unparalleled in its universal human quality, which is
derived from the inevitability of death and the resultant
sense of loss. However, as cultural and social anthro-
pologists have shown (see e.g. Scheper-Hughes 1993),

it manifests itself differently around the world, which makes it important to tread carefully when differentiating between general and particular aspects of grief. This has been particularly important in psychiatry in recent years, with the emergence of the diagnostic category 'complicated grief', which it is envisaged will have a broad validity that transcends cultures. Against this background, in Chapter 6 I return to the current debate about the medicalisation of grief and discuss the rationale behind the 'complicated grief' diagnosis. I look at the new grief diagnoses in the light of four authoritative theories of psychopathology, and conclude that although grief can be extremely painful, even debilitating, we do not yet have sufficient reason to believe that it is pathological in and of itself. In certain cases, grief may lead to mental disorders (particularly depression), but the trend toward medicalisation should, as far as possible, be resisted. The book concludes in Chapter 7 with a discussion of grief's status in contemporary cultural and social contexts.

It is worth noting that while the chapters collectively provide a holistic understanding of grief – from how it is experienced by the self, via phenomenology, to an understanding of the importance of body, sociality and materiality – they can also be read in isolation. Chapter 5, on the ecology of grief, is probably the most challenging, because it is the one that diverges the most clearly from the prevailing, individualistic understanding of grief. It may aid understanding to first read this introduction and then Chapter 7.

Science, art and culture

Although the book primarily seeks to convey general psychological perspectives on grief, I also wish to illustrate the discussion with references to various cultural and artistic idioms, including poetry and fiction (e.g. Joan Didion, Naja Marie Aidt), TV shows (e.g. *Black Mirror*), visual art (e.g. van Gogh, Munch) and theatre (both Greek tragedies and modern experimental drama). The point of this is not just to make the book more accessible. Rather, it reflects my conviction that art is more than an expression of an artist's irrational creative power, devoid of context – it is a systematic study of the many dimensions and phenomena of human experience, including grief. Science studies the world through its special methods and then conveys the results, but art does more than merely *narrate* – it also *shows* the phenomena being examined, which facilitates a more nuanced understanding than is possible with linear research methods. With this in mind, I hope that the book will prove useful to professionals in areas like psychology, psychiatry, philosophy, sociology, anthropology and theology, as well as to anyone interested in grief as a basic human experience. Although the book is primarily about grief as an emotion that usually follows the death of someone close, it also identifies grief as a basic existential state that is better encapsulated by art than by science. In his poetry collection *Rystet spejl* (Shaken Mirror), Søren Ulrich Thomsen writes of loss:

Little children too dream of their past
which is huge and dusky
full of scents and unrecognizable figures
reflected in polished floors.
Even the very old feel bereft
when they sit staring in dayrooms
and suddenly remember
that they have lost their parents.[3]

As human beings, the bonds we forge with others are both a gift and a curse – as such, grief is a lifelong companion. This mournful, melancholic undertone to life appears quite at odds with our positivity-oriented, happiness-obsessed age, and yet there is good reason to dwell on it, because it represents something deeply human. The sociologist Clive Seale has conducted detailed analyses of the significance of death and grief to society. As well as relating to the 'big grief' that follows a death, he also describes the 'little grief' that constantly lurks just below the surface in beings like us, who live in vulnerable bodies and know that death is an inescapable reality for us all (Seale 1998). Heidegger (1962), too, cast human existence as essentially 'being-toward-death'. We regularly experience minor senses of loss, for example when social bonds are broken in more or less dramatic ways. Seale writes that what we call grief is basically an extreme version of the 'everyday sadness' that confronts us when we try to turn our attention away from our finitude toward the business of getting on with our lives (Seale 1998: 211). Seale belongs to a group of sociologists and social psychologists who consider human knowledge of and respect for mortality to be an important foundation for the formation and maintenance of human society. He writes that all social

13

and cultural life is ultimately 'a human construction in the face of death'. For this reason, all social life is also 'a defense against the "grief" caused by realisation of embodiment' (1998: 8). The sociologist Peter Berger propounds a similar idea, that societies should be understood as consisting of people who have joined together in the face of death (referred to in Walter 1999: 21). Ernest Becker, in his classic 1973 book *The Denial of Death*, describes the fear of death as the main human condition and the engine behind social processes (Becker 2011). Hegel supposedly said a couple of centuries ago that, at its core, the history of the world is about the way in which humans relate to death (see Jacobsen 2016: 19). This book seeks to resurrect phenomenological thinking about the concept of existence and illustrate the relevance of phenomenology to social and psychological analyses, not least concerning the constitutive function of grief for both the self and society.

Grief's recent history

In keeping with its broadly phenomenological approach, the book's main aim is to explore the very being of grief. There is no easy answer to the question of the extent to which the essence of grief transcends cultures and eras. Nonetheless, the thesis of this book is that there is indeed something universal about what we refer to as grief, which means, for example, that we are able to understand the Greek tragedies, despite them being over 2,000 years old. At the same time, we need to remain mindful of the fact that there are, of course, many aspects of grief that do vary according to time and place, as we will see in the following chapters. I now conclude this introduction with a brief overview of the history of grief in my own part of the world, Denmark and the West, focusing on the last two centuries.

According to Horwitz and Wakefield, the oldest written reference to grief is found in the Babylonian epic *Gilgamesh*, from the third millennium BCE (Horwitz and Wakefield 2007: 30). When King Gilgamesh loses his friend Enkidu, his grief is described as highly intense – so much so that he coats himself with dirt and wanders restlessly through the desert. These feelings are quite recognisable to modern humans, many millennia later. An even more famous description of grief is provided by Homer 1,500 years later. In *The Iliad*, after losing his friend Patroclus, Achilles too covers himself with dirt, and tears out his hair. Kofod (2017) has drawn up a historical timeline for grief, starting with the ancient Greeks, for whom grief was considered a 'moral practice' and an essential part of human reason. For both Plato and Aristotle, the objective was for individuals to regulate their emotions in a manner proportionate to the situation. Later on, under the influence of Christianity, medieval culture endowed grief with a religious aspect. But perhaps the most significant change came in the nineteenth century, when Romanticism replaced the ancient and medieval 'cosmological grief' – directed outward toward a meaningful cosmic order – with 'inward grief', in which individuals engaged in dialogue with their inner selves. It was, in other words, a transition from cosmology to psychology.

In their account of historical perspectives on grief, Stearns and Knapp (1996) argue that grief reactions are, to a certain extent, cultural constructs. They also date the important historical shift in the perception of grief to the early nineteenth century, when the West's traditional (and previously relatively subdued) ways of expressing grief gave way to much more intense mourning practices, bordering on worship of grief, during the Victorian era. Although they appear natural, our modern grief responses, it is claimed, did not emerge until the early nineteenth century. The Victorian age is often thought of as a period of great self-control and suppression of desire, and yet expressions of grief were positively encouraged. Stearns and Knapp link this development in particular to the increasing importance of love in families, which had previously been purely practical units. Emotional ties between spouses – and between parents and children – were cultivated more intensely than before. At the same time, improvements in medical science facilitated the treatment of many more diseases and lowered mortality rates, particularly for children, far more of whom survived infancy. Poets started to write about death and grief, for both children and adults. Artistic expressions of grief were personal and immediate, as seen in this typical song from 1839:

> Mingled were our hearts forever, long time ago;
> Can I now forget her? Never. No, lost one, no.
> To her grave these tears are given, ever to flow.
> She's the star I missed from heaven, long time ago.[4]

It became increasingly common to dress in black and to spend money on funerals, with the wealthiest building lavish monuments to their dead. The sculptor William Wetmore Story's *Angel of Grief* (1894) is often seen as the culmination of the Victorian relationship to grief (even though Story was American). He produced it

The original *Angel of Grief* by William Wetmore Story
(1894)

after his wife's death, and it was his final sculpture. The original is in the Protestant Cemetery in Rome, but it is frequently copied.

Unlike earlier ornamentation of graves, which often sought to depict the deceased's life or portray angels in Heaven (what might be called outward grief, directed toward the cosmos), *Angel of Grief* expresses the grief of the bereaved (which is inward and psychological). It does so in what now seems an almost archetypal way – the angel has collapsed with her arms over her eyes and face (I will return to this sculpture in Chapter 4). Grief is, in every sense, a heavy emotion, and this weightiness is beautifully conveyed by Story's sculpture. Of course, the Anglo-Saxon world was not alone in defining grief in Victorian times, but Britain was a cultural superpower in those days, comparable with the

USA today. Nowadays, grief discourse is not shaped by English poets and sculptors, but by pop musicians and Hollywood film and TV directors.

The early years of the twentieth century saw a gradual rethink of the Victorian era's poetic and artistic idolisation of grief. Increasingly, it was considered preferable to conceal grief and move on. This trend was reinforced during the First World War, when expressing deep and lasting grief was considered weak and bad for morale. Throughout the twentieth century, Western countries gradually changed from industrial to consumer societies. Stearns and Knapp (1996) write that consumerism led to a further polarisation between positive and negative emotions, in which the former were to be supported and enacted. Conversely, the consumer society simply does not afford the same time for grief. People are expected to be flexible and adaptable, rather than mired in the past and maintaining their bonds with the dead. The second half of the twentieth century saw the emergence of a burgeoning happiness industry, in which emotional culture focused on the positive, on 'motivation' and 'passion' (Davies 2015). Grief was almost diametrically opposed to the feelings of proactivity and euphoria that were dominant and in demand. Psychologists and psychiatrists began systematically drawing up symptom checklists and formulating psychiatric diagnoses for ('complicated') grief, in order to ensure that nobody grieved needlessly and the bereaved were able to resume their social and work roles quickly.

In simple terms, in the last two centuries, grief in the West has changed from being a normal part of life, expressed mainly through religious practices and rituals, to a defining emotion of the Victorian age, when it was cultivated in art and literature and elaborate mourning practices emerged that were independent of the religious context. This started to change again with the first major war of the twentieth century. From that point on, grief became more contained and concealed, leading eventually to medicalisation. Right now, grief again appears to have become a central phenomenon, one through which human beings can be understood, especially via art and popular culture.

Parallel with the story of how grief is enacted and practised in different epochs is a corresponding account of how research into grief has changed. One of the earliest sources in the West was Robert Burton's *The Anatomy of Melancholy* (1651), in which the author interprets grief as a form of melancholia. However, he stresses that while melancholy is a disease of the mind, grief is a normal, melancholic response to loss (Granek 2010: 49). In 1872, Charles Darwin's *The Expression of the Emotions in Man and Animals* was published. In this famous work, Darwin briefly touches on grief and formulates a distinction between depression and grief, and between an active form of grief and a more passive, depressive form (Granek 2010: 50). John Shand was the first to conduct a proper psychological analysis of grief, in 1914 – interestingly, the year of the outbreak of the First World War – but it was Freud's analyses from roughly the same period that made the deepest impression on twentieth-century understandings of grief. Freud saw mental health and pathology as being on a continuum, and so did not think that there was a sudden leap from one extreme to the other. In his 1917 essay on grief and melancholy, he looked at what he saw as the core aim of 'grief work' (to use the psychodynamic term), which is helping the bereaved to redirect their emotional energy away from the deceased toward other aspects of life, and possibly a new loved one (Freud 2005). Freud also stressed that we should not see grief as a mental disorder and treat it with medicine or therapy. According to him, the difference between grief and melancholy (or depression, as we would say today) is simple – the former is understood within the context of loss; the latter does not involve loss and is, therefore, pathological. Phenomenologically speaking, depression is very close to grief, but without the element of loss. Or, in language closer to Freud's own: in grief, it is the world that has become empty, while in melancholia or depression it is the self.

The first significant pathologisation of grief was formulated by Helene Deutsch in 1937. She asserted that grief work can be abnormal, and may result in a chronic, pathological condition (Granek 2010: 53). However, she also considered *the absence* of grief after a loss to be pathological, introducing the idea of normal grief – neither too much nor too little – which would start to have an impact on research. A few years later, Melanie Klein and other psychoanalysts talked about grief as an actual illness. In the 1940s, Erich Lindemann conducted the first major empirical studies of grief among bereaved people (Granek 2010: 57). After interviewing more than 100 respondents, he concluded that grief was an illness, and a matter for medical science. Doctors were now advised to monitor patients' grief work, and later empirical studies by other researchers resulted in the same perspective on the phenomenon. In the 1960s, however, a critique of this strongly normative idea of grief work emerged. For example, in 1967, the anthropologist Geoffrey Gorer identified the cultural requirement to be happy as an obstacle to people grieving in ways more appropriate to their needs (Granek 2010: 61). In the late 1960s, Elisabeth Kübler-Ross also formulated the famous five stages of death and grief (isolation and denial, anger, bargaining, depression and acceptance). The jury is still out on whether it is reasonable to regard grief as a normative process in this way, but most contemporary scholars reject this view. It now appears that grief is much more individualised than any theories about phases or stages would imply (Guldin 2014).

There is also a more biological track in grief research, beginning with Darwin, and particularly associated with John Bowlby, a psychoanalyst who formulated an influential psycho-biological theory about the bonds between children and parents. This theory has also been deployed in research into patterns of grief. Colin Murray Parkes in particular has refined Bowlby's approach by conducting empirical studies of the process and of various interventions for complicated grief. Parkes (1998) summarised the grief research up to that point and grouped it into four leading types: (1) stress and crisis theories that explain grief as a stress reaction; (2) psychodynamic theories in the Freudian tradition; (3) attachment theories in the tradition of Bowlby; and (4) psychosocial theories about life transitions. Similarly, he identifies three basic models for the current scientific knowledge about grief: (I) phase models that attempt to describe the grief process in a more or less linear fashion; (II) the medical model, which looks at grief as a medical condition; and (III) the grief work model, which emphasises the importance of the bereaved person acknowledging their loss. All of these models have, however, been strongly criticised (Walter 1999: 103), and there is currently little consensus in the field. In a review, Leeat Granek concludes that, in the early 1990s, researchers were almost exclusively concerned with grief's dysfunctional nature. This book can be seen as an attempt to move in a different direction – one that stresses the idea that grief is existentially interesting in and of itself, and not only because of its possible clinical and pathological forms. According to Granek, the dominant themes of current research – which are *not* central to this book – are quantifying grief (the development of diagnostic symptom scales and lists); grief and trauma; continued discussion of the stages theory; individual differences in terms of grief reactions and mastering them; and above all else, complicated grief, in other words grief as an illness (Granek 2010: 65). While these themes are important, the focus in this book is on grief's very essence.

In addition to the changes in recent centuries in the practice of grief – and research into it during the same period – it is also relevant to mention changing relationships to death. Historically, far more research has been conducted into death than grief. The biggest name in the field is the French historian Philippe Ariès, who researched changing attitudes to death from the Middle Ages to modern times (Ariès 2009). He divided the history of death into the following epochs: *the tamed death* (the medieval approach, in which death was considered ubiquitous and familiar due to high levels of mortality and widespread rituals); *the death of self* (from the early Renaissance, when more elaborate ceremonies were introduced and the dying were even permitted to plan their death); *the death of the other* (the increasing alienation from death in modern society, and an increasing focus on the mourner, as discussed above in a Victorian context); and finally *the forbidden death* – a modern phenomenon, in which, according to Ariès, death is more taboo than ever. Death is now increasingly controlled and institutionalised in hospitals, separate from ordinary life. Grief is therefore, almost by necessity, more readily seen as a pathological condition to be treated, rather than a necessary experience governed by societal norms (see Jacobsen and Kofod 2015).

Jacobsen has recently proposed a new, fifth phase to Ariès' chronology, which he calls *the spectacular death*. In the twenty-first century, death is designed, staged and rendered spectacular to a greater extent than previously (Jacobsen 2016). Not in all cases, of course, but it can be identified as a significant historical shift away from the taboo that used to epitomise the modern era. Tony Walter has criticised the widespread notion of the death taboo, and in a new article speaks instead about *the pervasive dead* (Walter 2019). His contention is that the twenty-first century has witnessed the reintegration of death into everyday life. He bases this on a wide range of trends, including grief theories that emphasise continued bonds with the dead, digital memorials on social media, renewed interest in angels and the afterlife, and new funeral practices. He presents plenty of evidence to suggest that the widespread thesis of death as the last great taboo was at best oversimplified, and possibly even completely wrong.

Just as I began this chapter by referring to a series of cultural representations of grief, I could have done the same with regard to death. There are films and TV programmes about death, death cafés, and death features prominently as a theme in novels and visual art. The

23

history of death is, at its core, a story of what the focus has been in the management of the transition from life to death.[5] That focus shifted from the medieval concern for the soul and its salvation to early modernity's interest in the corpse (it was only slowly and gradually that scientists were allowed to examine dead bodies at all) (Walter 1999: 135). In modern times, the focus switches again, to interest in the bereaved. Grief practices are no longer primarily for the sake of the deceased – to ensure a good journey to the hereafter – but for the sake of the bereaved, to ensure a good psychological journey through the rest of their lives. This is probably most true in Protestant societies, which do not subscribe to a particular funerary theology (in the form of a sacrament or ritual to help the dead on their way to heaven) (Walter 1999: 33). In simple terms, we have moved from a *religious* culture to a *psychological* one; from *care for the soul of the deceased*, to care for the *psychological well-being of the bereaved*. This perspective is consistent with cultural analyses highlighting the fact that psychology has in many ways replaced religion for the individualised human being. In effect, psychologists are becoming more and more like the new priesthood, offering advice, relieving symptoms and aiding the development of the individual (Brinkmann 2014b).

Despite the background outlined above, this book will not explore the theme of death in depth, as it serves merely as a backdrop for an analysis of grief, for which death is a necessary precondition. However, it is valid – if unsurprising – to note that there are parallels between the developments over time in relation to both death and grief. In short, both show signs of increasing individualisation – away from fixed rituals and templates, to individual choices regarding death, burial and grieving practices. In extension of this, Tony Walter (1999: 207) has summarised the recent history of grief and divided it into three epochs:

- 1800–1950 (approx.): Early industrial society and Romantic culture. The Victorian era's aesthetic cultivation of grief, with a range of practices to maintain the memory of the dead.
- 1950–1980 (approx.): Complete modernity and technical rationality. Focus on 'grief work', standardised stage and phase theories and increasing medicalisation.
- 1980–present (approx.): Late capitalism and consumer society. Individualisation and subjectification of grief ('the customer is always right'), underlining that everybody grieves differently.

For Walter, the current conception of grief is torn between, on the one hand, a 'modern' understanding, where grief is framed by standardised theories about phases, and in which health systems are on hand with diagnoses and treatments for those who fall outside the normative frameworks; and on the other, a 'post-modern' understanding, in which grief is seen as an individual experience of suffering, which must be allowed to proceed free from the judgement of others. The post-modern understanding also includes the possibility of 'post-traumatic growth', i.e. that the experience of loss may give rise to existential reorientation and personal development. The problem with the former (the 'modern' understanding) is that it can be experienced as intrusive or even insulting when others relate normatively to our personal experience of loss and grief. The problem with the latter (the 'post-modern' understanding) is that it can entail a risk of the individual being abandoned, without fixed cultural templates and rituals to shape their personal grief.

Parkes and Prigerson share this concern, arguing that an agreed period of grief 'provides social sanction for beginning and ending grief, and it is clearly likely to have psychological value for the bereaved. . . . the absence of any social expectations, as is common in Western cultures today, leaves bereaved people confused and insecure in their grief' (Parkes and Prigerson 2010: 211). In other words, there is a risk of a kind of tyranny of formlessness, to use an expression taken from the Danish philosopher K.E. Løgstrup. Walter (1999: 119) notes dryly that when we look at all sorts of cultures, there is no society – save perhaps our own – where people are left alone with their grief.

The key question for our era, then, is whether people can grieve without a 'script' or 'template'. We might speculate whether the current debates about psychiatric diagnoses for complicated grief are based on a recognition that a definition of 'wrong' grieving becomes necessary when there is no general consensus about the grief process. Paradoxically, while diagnoses are essentially used to define the abnormal, they also provide new ways in which to be normal. It might be said that the diagnoses at least offer 'normal forms of abnormality', which may help in an era when norms are otherwise diffuse (Kofod 2015). I will return to this toward the end of the book. First, I will look at humans as creatures with the potential to grieve, at the phenomenology of grief, and at the role of the body and culture in the grieving process.

2

Grief as a Foundational Emotion

When human beings think about themselves in general terms – not as Peter, Paul or Mary, but as *human beings* – they usually make reference to rationality.[6] Biologically, humans are classified as *Homo sapiens*, which is Latin for 'wise man' or 'thinking person'. Around 2,500 years ago, Aristotle defined human beings as *zoon logikon* ('rational animal'). Early in the seventeenth century, René Descartes ushered in modern philosophy by claiming that we are essentially and uniquely a 'thinking thing' (*res cogitans*), whereas everything else in the universe consists merely of 'extended matter' (*res extensa*) (Descartes 2017). Historically, scientists and philosophers have often defined human beings by referring to rationality, as opposed to emotionality. Humans are thinking, intelligent, problem-solvers, traits thought to have been crucial to our ability to spread out over almost the whole of the planet and build complex societies and cultures. Nobody doubts that we also have feelings, but the prevailing scientific perspectives contend that these reflect the more primitive aspects of our nature that we share with other species, while rationality is the defining characteristic of humanity. Aristotle and Descartes are not the only ones to say so. A whole host of thinkers concur, from Antiquity via medieval philosophy to the Renaissance, the Enlightenment and modern philosophy. For example, in the late eighteenth century, Immanuel Kant (1998) described 'pure reason' as the preserve of humankind, arguing that our dignity and moral nature arise from reason, with no input from our feelings.

The above is, of course, a generalisation. There have always been competing views of human nature. Scholars have regularly questioned the related dualities of body and mind, and emotion and reason. This can be traced all the way back to Aristotle (1976), who interpreted emotions as rational. As will become clear, this book shares that perspective on emotions – namely that feelings such as grief at the passing of a loved one are a source of knowledge, and not just an irrational, affective event in an organism. Leading contemporary research into emotions, including by the neuroscientist Antonio Damasio, also asserts that the links between emotion and reason are closer than is generally acknowledged within the philosophical tradition. While Aristotle believed that emotions were (at least partly) rational, Damasio stresses that reason is always also (at least partly) emotional, if it is to result in rational actions in specific situations (Damasio 1994). When we consider theories of how the individual is constituted – i.e. as an individual self, and not just in terms of universally human features – we realise that our feelings, and the entirety of the affective dimension of our lives, have played a much larger role than is allowed for in more general categorisations of what it means to be human.[7]

I believe that we can reasonably say that different philosophical, religious and scientific anthropologies (i.e. basic theories about human beings) usually operate on the basis of different *foundational emotions*.

The concept of foundational emotions is my own invention, and has its own specific meaning. It is not the same as *basic emotions* – a psychological concept associated with Paul Ekman's longstanding efforts to draw up a basic register of emotional expressions that are visible in the human face and allegedly universal across cultures. According to Ekman (1992), this register consists of basic emotions such as anger, disgust, fear, happiness, sadness and surprise. I adopt a neutral stance on the otherwise widespread discussion about the universality of such emotions. While many scholars argue that basic emotions are universal, others think that there is great cultural variation, or claim that the distinction between basic and non-basic emotions is inherently problematic, because small children express many more emotions than the few included on Ekman's list (Draghi-Lorenz, Reddy and Costall 2001). Notwithstanding the importance of these basic emotions, I use the concept of foundational emotions to identify something else – that a basic sensitivity is constitutive of the human self, the *uniquely* human self. No other creatures in the known universe have these emotions – only humans. I use the term foundational because they form the basis for the reflexive human self – they are the foundation of the self. Alternatively, we might say that the self is either founded through these emotions or underpinned by the ever-present ability to feel them. This does not mean that the self (which I will home in on below) is a purely emotional matter that has nothing to do with reason. Rather, when discussing the human self, it is impossible to draw a sharp boundary between rationality and emotionality.

This chapter introduces and discusses in depth this idea of foundational emotions. First, I will present and endorse a particular theory of emotions, and then outline examples of three emotions that, at different points in history, have been considered foundational (albeit without this specific term being used about them): *anxiety*, *shame* and *guilt*, as articulated by Søren Kierkegaard, the Bible (and Katz 1996) and Friedrich Nietzsche (and Butler 2005), respectively. In all three cases, there is reason to believe that it is the human capacity to experience this specific feeling that makes it possible to be a self in the human sense. I will then add *grief* to this list of foundational emotions. Unlike the more general 'sadness', which is on Ekman's list, grief is not usually considered a basic emotion. However, I will argue that it is a foundational one, in the sense that it places the human subject in a unique relationship to the existential themes of love and death that we do not see in other species. In the previous chapter, we saw this expressed by the poet Søren Ulrik Thomsen, who articulates a kind of fundamental grief related to human temporal existence. Time passes, and humans are aware of this in a different and deeper way than other animals, which are tied more immediately to the present. As we grow older, our thoughts may return, perhaps suddenly and involuntarily, to those we have lost – parents, siblings and friends. This kind of existential grief is not an accidental feature of our lives, but reflects a foundational emotion that is constitutive of reflexive selfhood in a relationship to love and death. That, in brief, is the thesis of this chapter. It has also been expressed by scholars such as Leeat Granek, who describes it beautifully as 'an affective thread that moves across societies, institutions, communities, and relationships' (2013: 283). We should learn to relate to this thread as a basic element interwoven into the whole of our lives. Animals appear to lack this thread, because they are tied to the immediate present. They do not relate to time in the same way as human beings, nor do they spin threads to others as we do.

What are emotions?

Before proceeding to the analyses of foundational emotions, it will be helpful to provide a more general definition of emotions. This is a key issue that recurs throughout the book, and, as we go on, I will seek to refine the understanding of emotions generally and of grief specifically. However, even at this early stage, we encounter difficulties, because psychologists, philosophers, sociologists, neuroscientists and others all disagree strongly on the issue. Nonetheless, there is broad consensus that humanities research has undergone an 'affective turn' in recent years, which has seen the traditional interest in knowledge, thinking and perception supplemented by (and sometimes even replaced by) a focus on the whole affective spectrum of human life (Wetherell 2012). As a result, any definition of emotions is likely to reflect a particular theoretical perspective. According to the definition used by advocates of *appraisal theory*, emotions are an organism's 'adaptive responses which reflect appraisals of features of the environment that are significant for the organism's well-being' (Moors et al. 2013:

31

119). This definition, to which I will return repeatedly, is based on the appraisal theories that originated with Aristotle and were brought up to date by Magda Arnold (1960), Richard Lazarus (1991) and others from the 1960s onwards. These theories emphasise that feelings (still understood as emotions) include aspects of appraisal and judgement – namely, of what is important for an organism or a person. While these judgements are not purely static, they serve as transactional processes between the organism and the environment; as such, feelings are understood as *episodes* or *processes*, rather than *states*. Emotional processes consist of changes in a range of physiological and psychological components. For appraisal theorists, an emotion is a syndrome made up of motivational, somatic, motor, sensation and appraisal components. There are sensations that are not feelings – external ones, such as how the surface of an object feels when we touch it, as well as internal ones like nausea – and there are feelings that are not accompanied by characteristic sensations, such as the fear that interest rates will rise or the modest pride felt in a job well done.

In a similar vein, the philosopher and psychologist Rom Harré (2009) has argued that emotions should be understood as hybrids of cognitive (knowledge), affective (the senses) and somatic (the body) elements. The cognitive component is what the definition above calls an appraisal. If we put our hand on a hot cooker, we will feel immediate pain, but this involves no cognitive judgement, and therefore no feeling (in the sense of emotion). A burning sensation in the hand is not in itself an emotion. An appraisal corresponds to passing judgement. It does not need to be based on a long interpretation process, but can be a rapid response to a given situation. Anger, for example, is inseparable from the appraisal that someone, in some way or other, has violated my rights, just as grief is inseparable from the knowledge that a loved one has passed away. Harré immediately issues a warning about the excessive reification of feelings. When we talk about anger or grief, it is easy to talk about them as actually existing in the world. This invariably leads us to the question: where are they? In the brain? In the body? In our relationships? Harré considers these questions flawed, because they are rooted in an illegitimate reification of emotionality. In reality, of course, it is human beings who have these feelings. The words 'anger' or 'grief' do not refer to anything in and of themselves. It is more fruitful to express the concepts of emotions in their adverbial or adjectival forms, talking about a person 'acting angrily' or behaving 'like a grieving daughter', for example. Although it is possible to use nouns to allude to feelings, it is important not to imply that they refer to phenomena in the world that are separate from the actions of the individual. Harré advocates that we strive to perceive emotions as being more analogous with 'to go' (an activity) than with 'digestion' (an event). Digestion takes place in the organism, as a causal process that is situated specifically in the peristaltic system, whereas to go somewhere is something that a person *does* (it does not just *happen* as a passive event). It makes little sense to ask where the going is localised. Is it the legs that go? The feet? The shoes? No, it is, of course, the human being as an indivisible entity (an individual) who goes. This does not imply that the person's body is irrelevant. The same also applies to feelings – it is a person who grieves, not their brain, eyes, arms or legs. Grief does not exist as a discrete, separate entity in the world, but there are, of course, people in grief, people who are *grieving*.

In addition to an appraisal, an altered physical condition and sensory changes – the first of these being the most important for the individual's ability to identify their feelings – Harré underlines the importance of emotions' *action tendencies*. If we do not have a tendency to avoid what we fear, then it is not fear in a meaningful sense. If we do not have a tendency to want to avenge an injustice, then what we are feeling is not anger. There is no simple, one-to-one relationship between emotion and action – partly because the emotion itself, according to Harré, should be understood adverbially as a form of doing – but there are characteristic impulses to act associated with the different emotions, just as there are characteristic changes in the face, the body and the senses. However, it must again be stressed that the cognitive or appraising component takes precedence. The other components can be added to or subtracted from an emotion, but a bodily change without an appraisal of the situation is not a real emotion. At best, it is an amorphous agitation, dejection or similar. The appraisal is a necessary condition for emotions, but rarely enough on its own – other aspects are needed as well (bodily, mimetic, sensory and so on). Often, mental disorders are characterised by just such an amorphous experience. For example, the feeling of fear is completely understandable when it occurs just before a parachute jump, but if we experience the same bodily and sensory changes without being able to attribute them to a terrifying situation, it may be more appropriate to classify the response as a mental disorder. Similarly, in terms of bodily sensations and feelings, depression is close to grief – but without an identifiable loss it is not grief, just depression as a mental disorder. It is primarily the appraisal and recognition of conditions in our environment that determines the nature of the emotion.

Many theories of emotion emphasise the importance of the immediate affective response (e.g. Zajonc 1984). However, this book supports those theories that emphasise the cognitive basis. The influential philosopher Martha Nussbaum elaborates one such theory in her *magnum opus* on emotions. She writes that emotions 'are not just the fuel that powers the psychological mechanism of a reasoning creature, they are parts, highly complex and messy parts, of this creature's reasoning itself' (2001: 3). Her book is called *Upheavals of Thought*, the title of which hints at the close relationship between our thoughts and our emotions regarding events in the world. In it, she develops a sophisticated theory based on Aristotelian and Stoic insights into the links between values, appraisals and emotions, but does not neglect the bodily, organism-oriented aspects of our emotions.

Central to the phenomenological appraisal theory expounded in this book is the *intentionality* of emotional life. Emotions refer to something in the world – they are, in their own way, *about something*. They are not simply physiological states or processes – abstract inner feelings or sensations – but possess the key quality of intentionality. In a very broad sense, emotions express and illuminate a person's attachment to objects that are beyond the individual's full control. According to Nussbaum, feelings (again understood as emotions) entail 'a certain sort of vision or recognition, as value-laden ways of understanding the world' (2001: 88). This understanding of feelings, i.e. as an acknowledging activity analogous to sight, enables us to order them based on the specific nature of the relationship between the person and the object (here, object is meant in a very broad sense, including other people). We feel joy when the coveted object is at hand; fear when it is threatened; grief when it is lost; gratitude when someone does something good for the object; anger when it is damaged; envy when someone else has it; and jealousy when somebody has a closer relationship with it, etc. (Nussbaum 2001: 87).

If emotions have this core characteristic of *intentionality* (being externally directed toward the world), this also means that they are *normative* in at least two senses:

(1) Emotions are normative in the sense that they can be more or less *reliable* ways of understanding the world around us. Righteous anger tells us that legitimate rights have been violated. However, we can, of course, also feel unjustified anger. Similarly, legitimate pride may tell us that we have done something commendable (although, again, pride may also be unjustified if a goal was achieved by using dishonest means). As Harré argued many years ago, the reason why phenomena such as exhaustion and constipation are classified as physiological, whereas anger and pride are classified as psychological, is that the latter belong to a normative, moral order (Harré 1983). Unlike physiological phenomena, which arise mechanically in the body as reactions to causal processes, feelings (like other types of psychological phenomena) are responsive – they are something people *do* or *perform* in specific situations – and as such they can be done more or less correctly and

adequately. Human thoughts can be more or less valid and informative about events in the world, and the same applies to emotions. Emotions do not tell us *what* is happening in the world, but rather *how* it happens. For example, I may know the 'what fact' that seven armed men are pointing guns at me, because I can use my rational faculties to count to seven, but the 'how fact', that these men are dangerous and threatening, depends on my emotional understanding of the situation. Again, we see that emotions involve an understanding of the world that may be more or less correct in the normative sense.

(2) This brings us to the second sense in which emotions are normative – they can be assessed relative to standards of correctness. In everyday life, we praise and rebuke people for their emotions, which would be unfair if emotions were simply a matter of causality, like physiological phenomena, without any agency. If, for example, I become angry with a small child because she spills milk, my anger is normatively wrong (because it is disproportionate), and others may rightly chide me for it. An important part of human socialisation consists of teaching children which emotions are correct in which situations and in relation to which objects (this normative approach to emotion can be traced back to Aristotle). In that sense, emotions are a way of understanding a situation, and as such they are subject to moral judgement. For example, if a child is given a present that he or she does not want (say, clothes instead of a toy) and reacts by yelling and screaming, most parents will, quite rightly, point out to the child that the giver's intentions were generous. In this way, the child learns that a sense of gratitude is a normatively valid

response to the situation, rather than a sense of anger and grievance – although it can be difficult to convey this to a child in the moment. Nonetheless, learning to feel gratitude indicates that the child has a deeper under-standing of the situation, which they would otherwise not attain if they were permitted to act impulsively, with anger. A sense of genuine gratitude conveys information about the situation that was not otherwise obvious.

The characteristics of human emotions mentioned so far – that they are intentional, evaluative and themselves the subject of evaluation (hence the normative aspect) – are difficult, if not impossible, to grasp from the per-spective of what Zinck and Newen refer to as 'feeling theories', which 'individuate emotions by their subjec-tive phenomenal content' (2008: 3). In other words, according to these theories it is possible to distinguish one feeling from another on the basis of how it *sub-jectively feels*. However, while a range of emotions are associated with specific bodily sensations (a knot in the stomach when afraid, or feeling like a volcano on the brink of eruption when angry), it is problematic to make them the essence of emotions. Humility, respect, admi-ration, contempt and gratitude, for example, are not generally felt in the body – they cannot be identified by a bodily state (Bennett and Hacker 2003: 205). They are better understood via cognitive theories, in which emotions are differentiated from each other by how the individual thinks about the world (i.e. their judge-ments), rather than internal, bodily changes. This line of thought – one endorsed by this book – begins with Aristotle and continues all the way up to Schachter and Singer's (1962) famous psychological experiments that demonstrated the significance of background beliefs for how individuals interpret physiological changes. They found that bodily changes induced by hormone injections can be interpreted differently – as expressions of either positive arousal or negative anger – depending on the situation in which the change is experienced. It is not the bodily changes themselves that constitute a particular emotion, but the person's own appraisal of what caused the changes. These experiments have proven difficult to reproduce, but they have given rise to what is referred to as the two-factor theory of emotion, in which (1) an amorphous bodily change only becomes real in a psychological sense when it is (2) interpreted cognitively with reference to the situation in which the individual finds themselves. Later constructionist theories, as well as the abovementioned appraisal theories of emotion, have increasingly downplayed the physiological element, and tend to see feelings merely as an expression of the individual's appraisal of a situation. However, the twist in this theoretical tail is the evidence suggesting that the individual's appraisals are not generated by disembodied intellects, but involve a bodily being-in-the-world. In other words, it may indeed be possible to take physicality into account by 'embodying' appraisal theories. I will return to this in Chapter 4, but in the meantime, suffice to say that this book will continue to follow the appraisal tradition in studies of emotions.

Before looking at examples of emotions that have been declared to be foundational (constitutive of the self), we will briefly touch on the work of the renowned philosopher Robert Solomon (2007), which includes a useful list of common myths about emotions. Like Aristotle and Nussbaum, Solomon believes that our emotions are based on rationality. They do not just 'happen', as passive events in a physiological system, but are 'done' or performed by individuals in response to specific situations. Emotions are, therefore, one of the keys to ethical judgement, and we have a certain indisputable responsibility for them. They provide the basis upon which we learn to orientate ourselves in the world and with other people, writes Solomon (2007: 217). He goes on to correct eight widespread misunderstandings and myths about feelings:

(1) Emotions are ineffable and beyond language: No, we can describe our feelings to each other and put ourselves in the shoes of others. Indeed, this is one of literature's essential functions. We are not 'trapped' in our subjective emotions, but have a general immediate understanding of other people's emotions.

(2) Emotions are feelings: No, this ignores the absolutely crucial element of intentionality – that feelings (in the sense of emotions) are directed toward objects in the world around us.

(3) Emotions are a kind of 'fuel': No, this a misleading metaphor that ignores the fact that emotions are organised and cultivated in social contexts. It is not just a matter of filling the tank!

(4) Emotions are 'in the mind': No, emotions are expressions of what is important to people and are linked to the way in which they cope with situations. Such phenomena are not located 'in the mind', but are a way of being in the world that involves the whole person's physical body, culture and social relations.

(5) Emotions are stupid: No, on the contrary, they are intelligent ways of understanding differences, including between what is dangerous and harmless, joyful and

sad, and so on. However, emotions are, of course, only wise if the person's emotional life has been cultivated adequately during their upbringing.

(6) Emotions are either positive or negative: No, except in the most superficial way. It is not negative to react with grief when a loved one dies. Instead, it is an expression of an understanding of the dead person's importance. The mere fact that something hurts is not the same as it being negative.

(7) Emotions are irrational: No, emotions are about achieving a correct understanding of the world. This is a rational ability, not an irrational one. This does not mean that the ability is always managed successfully, but that is no different than for other mental activities that do not always result in wise thoughts, or than for perception, which does not always provide a true picture of the world.

(8) Emotions are mental processes that happen to us: No, and this is perhaps the crucial misunderstanding. As mentioned, emotions are an active part of our lives – not in the sense that we can completely manage and control them, but perhaps in a similar way to our thoughts or speech. When we think a thought or say something to anybody else, words flow from us in a manner that is not always conscious. I hear what I am saying to somebody at the same time they hear it. I then calibrate my next sentence based on what I am hearing myself say, and on the other's reactions. This whole process is often accompanied by an emotional response. In other words, it is often difficult to distinguish between a rational understanding of a situation or conversation, and an emotional understanding – and this is precisely the point.

We hold ourselves and each other accountable for our emotions. This implies that emotions do not just happen – they are not mere reflexive responses that are beyond our control – but are part of our active life. We might scold someone for excessive anger or a cold response to an event that calls for emotional warmth. We can praise someone for a well-developed emotional life that means they possess a kind of practical wisdom and an ability to understand other people and their situations. This is a central point in Solomon's phenomenology of emotions, and one supported by this book. As for grief, Solomon writes explicitly that it is a way to keep love alive when the object of it has departed. He describes it as a 'moral emotion', because it is not only an appropriate response to death, but one that is almost obligatory (2007: 75). As we will discuss later in the book, there is a very strong normative impetus to grieve. This is true of all emotion, but it is particularly significant in the case of grief, given its location in the existential space between love and death.

Foundational emotions

As humans we have an extensive register of emotions at our disposal, which we use to recognise value-laden aspects of the world. We appear to share many of our emotions with other animals. The question of whether human emotions are truly unique is a complex one, and there is much debate about the extent of human exceptionalism. I do not delve any deeper into it here, except to say that I agree with those who say that some emotions are indeed specific to humans. My dog is undoubtedly overjoyed when I come home, and scared when it thunders, but I do not believe that he feels more complex moral emotions such as pride or shame. I am aware that many dog owners would reject this, and claim that their dog clearly feels shame when scolded. However, even though it looks like shame when a dog crawls along the ground with their ears back, this is in fact a sign of submission rather than actual shame, because dogs lack the requisite selfhood to feel shame (Gaita 2005). In their major work on philosophy and neuroscience, which also includes an in-depth discussion of emotional life, Bennett and Hacker concur with this, and argue that non-human animals' cognitive and emotional capacities are limited by their lack of language in particular.

From this perspective (which I share), emotions are ways in which living beings express what is important to them. Animals can do this to a certain extent, but 'human beings characteristically reflect on what matters to them, whereas non-language-using animals merely manifest what they care about (their territory, possession of the prey they have killed, their dominance in their group, etc.)' (Bennett and Hacker 2003: 206). Since some emotions presuppose reflexivity and the linguistic mastery of certain concepts, it is logically impossible for animals who lack such mastery to experience emotions such as guilt, remorse and moral indignation. I would also add to this list anxiety (but not fear, as per the discussion below), shame (but not submission, which certain animals do show) and grief (but not separation anxiety).

While many non-human animals undoubtedly have a basic emotional repertoire (which varies according to species), I believe that what I call foundational emotions are different, since they involve language, substantial reflexivity and self-awareness. Acquiring the capacity for these emotions is in a sense akin to becoming a fully rounded human subject. Monique Scheer has explored the links between emotions and subjectivity by ana-lysing emotions as a particular form of practice (i.e. patterns in what people *do*, rather than something they *have*). She concluded that 'the feeling subject is not prior to but emerges in the doing of emotion' (2012: 220). Below, we look at the emotions that, over time, have been identified as foundational to human subjectivity, i.e. constitutive of the reflexive self.

Anxiety

When Søren Kierkegaard was writing in Denmark in the first half of the nineteenth century, the world was on the cusp of modernity, with all of the individualism, meaninglessness and loneliness that came with it. His labyrinthine works, written under a host of pseudonyms and in multiple voices, articulated various existential positions on religious, ethical and psychological ques-tions. In *The Concept of Anxiety* he wrote (as Vigilius Haufniensis) of anxiety as a uniquely human emo-tion. Unlike fear, which we share with animals, and which has a specific object, anxiety has no such object (Kierkegaard 1980). Above, I asserted that emotions are intentional, they are *about something*. However, anxi-ety is particularly fascinating because, at least according to Kierkegaard, it is about *nothing*. We may rightly fear a dangerous animal – just as a weaker animal may fear a stronger one – but anxiety is not directed at such a specific phenomenon. For Kierkegaard, anxiety is not a physical or mental phenomenon, but a spiritual one, a category of experience that designates how the relationship between body and mind relates to itself. Anxiety is, therefore, uniquely human, because it presupposes an understanding of the concept of nothingness, including as a form of freedom. In this way, anxiety is inextricably linked with the human capacity for reflexive selfhood, and as such can be classified as a foundational emotion. Kierkegaard writes:

> When it is stated in Genesis that God said to Adam, 'Only from the tree of the knowledge of good and evil you must not eat,' [as to do so would be to gain an understanding of good and evil] it follows as a matter of course that Adam really has not understood this word, for how could he understand the difference between good and evil when this distinction would follow as a consequence of the enjoyment of the fruit? (1980: 44)

It is the case, therefore, that '[the] prohibition induces in him anxiety, for the prohibition awakens in him freedom's possibility. What passed by innocence as the nothing of anxiety has now entered into Adam, and here again it is a nothing – the anxious possibility of *being able*' (Kierkegaard 1980: 44). While I do not believe in Genesis as a historical account, I think that the tale contains a profound psychological truth: that the ability to make an informed choice – should I do it or not? – is linked to fear. This fear is targeted precisely at the non-realised, at the possibility of acting – or not acting (this is also a theme in Brinkmann 2016c). Unlike animals, which act on the strongest impulse at any given time, humans can take a step back and appraise their impulses – not least, in the light of moral values. According to

Kierkegaard, it is fear that produces the capacity to engage in this kind of reflection. As such, this feeling is intimately intertwined with morality and the human self. That is the first psychological truth in Genesis (the second will follow soon).

But what is this self that is constituted through fear? The famous introduction to *The Sickness Unto Death* – written under the pseudonym Anti-Climacus, but published under the name S. Kierkegaard – explains this:

> Man is spirit. But what is spirit? Spirit is the self. But what is the self? The self is a relation which relates itself to its own self, or it is that in the relation [which accounts for it] that the relation relates itself to its own self; the self is not the relation but [consists in the fact] that the relation relates itself to its own self. (Kierkegaard 1954: 146)

This quote is not quite as impenetrable as it first appears. Firstly, Kierkegaard defines humankind as spirit, and asks what exactly spirit is. His response – that spirit is the self – immediately leads to a new problem, that of defining the self. He determines that the self is a relation that relates to itself. In other words, the self is not an object or substance, but a relation. But between what? As previously mentioned, the answer is between mind and body. Humans are, to use the language of Kierkegaard's day, the synthesis of soul and body. However, the mere fact of a relation between soul and body – the psychological and the physiological – does not constitute a self in the Kierkegaardian sense. This relation only becomes spiritual, and thus a self, in the act of relating to itself. In other words, the self is neither our psyche nor our biological body, nor the sum of those parts, but the act of relating to the synthesis (or relation) between the two.

The self, therefore, is the process in human life by which we relate not only to our psyche, body or the world in general, but also to *how* we relate to all of these things. It is, in other words, our capacity for (self-)reflection. While it may sound strange, Kierkegaard argues that this ability is based on a foundation of anxiety.

In psychology, this perspective was in a sense developed by Freud (1990), who portrayed human beings as creatures who are constantly employing defence mechanisms to protect themselves from anxiety. Like Kierkegaard, Freud thought that prohibitions trigger anxiety by dint of the urge to defy them, hence the defence mechanism. In both Kierkegaard and Freud, the formula is as follows: prohibitions lead to anxiety because people want to defy them. Kierkegaard's point is that the reflexive self, which can choose to act or not – and which it is, therefore, relevant to judge in moral terms – is rooted in the anxiety triggered by a prohibition that tears the subject out of their immediacy and creates a reflexive distance to their own desires. Kierkegaard gave us a general structural analysis of this phenomenon, and Freud tried to account for its ontogenesis, i.e. psychological development dynamics. While there may be certain gaps and partial errors in their accounts (especially in Freud), I believe the overarching insight remains valid – that anxiety is a foundational emotion for the human self.

Shame

In both Kierkegaard and Genesis, another foundational emotion quickly enters the picture. As we have seen, Kierkegaard interprets the biblical story of Creation as informing us about the existential anxiety that humans feel in response to nothingness (in terms of the possibility of freedom). It is this anxiety that turns humanity away from immediacy and innocence, and toward reflexive selfhood. However, this selfhood is also intimately linked to shame. Jack Katz's social-psychological reading positions Genesis as 'an experiment in theoretical imagination that produces a highly compressed social psychology' (1996: 557). Genesis is a social-psychological description of how the human self is born in shame, precisely 'because it is a brief description of the challenges people face in their relations with others' (1996: 559–60). The myth teaches us that the self is born as a reflexive process, when a person sees themselves through the eyes of another, and that this is a shameful moment (Madsen and Brinkmann 2012). In Genesis, shame is associated with the emergence of self-reflection – and thus of the fully developed human self. When Adam and Eve recognise that they have done something wrong by disobeying the word of God, they see that they are naked, feel shame, and that they must cover their bodies. This shame is reinforced when God gives them clothes and banishes them from Paradise.

In Masaccio's famous fresco from 1425, we see how Adam and Eve adopt universal gestures of shame – covering their eyes and genitalia, respectively, to shield themselves from the gaze of others and of God. As will be expanded upon below, there are certain similarities between the bodily expressions of shame and of grief. Before they ate of the tree of knowledge, Adam and Eve symbolically reached up toward the branches of the tree of wisdom, lured by the wily serpent on the ground. The forbidden fruit, writes Katz, is 'the very process of self-

Masaccio, *The Expulsion Of Adam and Eve from Eden*
(1425)

conscious reflection' (1996: 549). In this way, shame becomes another foundational emotion that constitutes the human self in its relationship to a community and a moral order. Scheff (2003) corroborates this in his sociological analysis of shame as a 'master emotion', as he calls it, which is linked directly to the social bonds between people. In light of psychological and sociological theory, the Genesis myth does seem to serve as a succinct account of the emergence of the human self and its unique capacity for reflection and moral capability. It articulates the important idea that the self is linked to the possibility of feeling shame, when we see ourselves as others see us. An archetypal example of shame, therefore, is when someone looking through a keyhole discovers that they are also being observed by others (Karlsson and Sjöberg 2009). In this example, the self is painfully objectified. This bodily sensation of being vulnerable and exposed is captured accurately in Masaccio's old fresco. In shame, the person is unable to control the way in which they are presented to others. It is, therefore, a powerful social control mechanism. Almost paradoxically, in this painful *revelation* of the self, it (the self) is simultaneously *created* as a reflexive product – in a way, it is created *in* and *by* the very revelation.

Guilt

A third emotion worth highlighting as foundational is guilt. Guilt is close to shame in many ways, but whereas the latter is related to a painful revelation of the self, guilt usually stems from a tangible act or transgression committed by the individual. In psychological terms, guilt's function is to tell us that we have done something wrong – such as broken a promise (see Brinkmann 2016c). People have long sought to rid themselves of guilt. Both guilt and shame can certainly be problematic, in the sense that people can have these emotions for no good reason, even if they have not done anything wrong, e.g. people who have suffered abuse as children. In such situations, it is important to realise that there is absolutely no reason to harbour these negative emotions. Sometimes the opposite is true – we do not feel guilt, even though we have done something wrong (again, the normativity of emotions becomes clear). In situations like those, we may not even realise that we have done something wrong, precisely because we lack the guilt that would otherwise highlight the transgression. Like the other foundational emotions, guilt can serve as a moral compass, without which it is difficult to act morally. For this reason, it is important that children learn to feel guilt when they are guilty (but not, of course, when they are innocent).

Guilt acts both as moral compass and as a form of emotional glue that keeps our moral life together. This may explain why we never really seek to rid ourselves of it, despite the fact that it can be extremely painful. In his 1973 novel *Manden der ville være skyldig* (The Man Who Wanted to Be Guilty), Henrik Stangerup mounts a literary defence of the existential importance of guilt. The book is set in a dystopian society ruled by therapists, where people are valued, accepted and understood – even if, like the protagonist, they have murdered their spouse. The man tries to be found guilty, but in a society where people have been deprived of personal responsibility, guilt has no meaning. Stangerup's analysis remains highly relevant today, in our psychology-based and therapy-ridden culture, which often emphasises positivity and recognition over guilt and shame.

Nietzsche, in particular, wrote about guilt as constitutive of the self – a notion that Judith Butler has made topical again in recent times. She believes that it is essential to our concept of a human being (she talks about 'the subject') that they are capable of giving 'accounts' of what they do. Usually, people are able to justify their actions – at least to the extent that they have acquired language. According to Butler (2005), it is primarily through moral relations that the subject is created, rather than the other way around, as is often asserted in our individualistic culture – i.e. that subjects choose their morality once they are fully formed. This is erroneous, Butler argues, as there is no real subjectivity prior to or independent of morality, nor is there any subjectivity prior to or independent of power (as Foucault also claimed). We start to exist as human beings when we are asked – or forced – by others to account for our actions. We start to be able to relate to ourselves when others intervene in our lives and insist that we explain ourselves in relation to moral norms. If we are never asked to account for ourselves, we remain in a state of immediacy, unable to develop reflexive self-consciousness.

Butler refers to Nietzsche, who believed that the reflexive subject arises through, as he rather dramatically put it, 'fear and terror' (Butler 2005: 11). By this, he means that we begin to account for our actions the moment that we are asked to do so by someone in a position of authority (e.g. a parent or teacher) within a sanctioned system of laws and punishments. Children encounter the requirement to account for themselves when they do something wrong or forbidden (spilling milk for example), and their parent asks, angrily, 'Why on earth did you do that?' They may not know why they did it, but they are still required to account for or justify their (unfortunate) behaviour. The adults address them as if they are morally responsible beings, even before they are – and it is precisely this that helps them *become* morally responsible beings. In this context, guilt is extremely important. As Butler puts it, 'the accusation of guilt produces the possibility of a subject' (2005: 85). The accusation of guilt draws the child into a relationship in which they are more or less forced to evaluate themselves and their actions, as part of a process that determines their guilt or innocence. Nobody becomes a morally responsible being overnight or following a single accusation of guilt – rather, it is a process that takes years, during which we gradually cultivate our subjectivity, creating self-reflexive individuals capable of accounting for ourselves. If Butler and Nietzsche are right, the reflexive self that assumes responsibilities is inconceivable without both the guilt itself and the breach of the moral order that the guilt acknowledges.

Grief as a foundational emotion

The point of looking at anxiety, shame and guilt as foundational emotions is not to argue that one of them is primary and the others secondary. Rather, it is that our capacity to have these emotions forms the foundation of human subjectivity. They inform human beings about the possibility of freedom (in the case of anxiety), the moral order of a community (shame), and personal responsibility (guilt). It is fair to say that all of these phenomena, in their own way, are at the heart of human existence. Interestingly, they are also examples of what researchers often refer to as 'negative' emotions, but as we saw with Solomon, this does not mean that they are bad per se and should be avoided. It simply means that there is considerable pain and discomfort associated with them, even though they are helpful in terms of making us aware of significant objects and values in the world. It is a tragic aspect of the human condition that these 'negative' foundational emotions are the price we pay for reflexive selfhood and moral capabilities. Without them, we could not develop the kind of moral agency that many see as defining humanity.

In the last part of this chapter, I argue that grief should be added to the list of foundational emotions. While grief, too, can be considered a negative emotion – simply because it is painful – it is usually, and correctly, also considered a deeply meaningful response to loss. It is not usually an emotion we associate with ethical norms. Rather, grief is, as is often stated, the price we pay for love. This adds an important dimension to our understanding of the human condition that is not immediately obvious in anxiety, shame or guilt – our capacity to form lasting, committed interpersonal relationships. The three other foundational emotions focus on our capacity as moral beings, but grief is also concerned, in a more direct way, with the fact that we live our lives in networks of committed, emotional relationships with specific others, for whom we grieve when they die.

As mentioned earlier, grief has been the subject of much public debate in recent years, partly due to the ongoing pathologisation of the phenomenon (Brinkmann

2016a). This is evident from the new diagnoses 'complicated grief disorder' and 'prolonged grief disorder', which are included in the international diagnostic systems DSM and ICD. I return to these in Chapter 6, which deals with grief as a mental disorder. Since all cultures have particular ways of interpreting and expressing grief (Kofod 2017), the question is, of course, what happens when this basic existential phenomenon is transformed into a psychiatric category. If it is reasonable to regard grief as a foundational emotion, it must be the case – just as for anxiety, shame and guilt – that it is specifically linked to reflexive human selfhood. Again, debate rages about whether non-human species feel grief. As mentioned earlier, an understanding of love and death is a prerequisite for grief, and animals appear to lack this understanding. Nussbaum (2001: 89) cites examples of other mammals that express emotions resembling intense grief, but I believe that those feelings are better understood as separation anxiety – for example, dogs feel that something is missing when their owners are away. Dogs do not reflect on the inevitability of death, because to do so would require them to understand the concept of death. Adopting an evolutionary perspective on grief, Archer concludes that 'of all animal species, only humans of a particular developmental age can understand the significance of death, and therefore respond differently to bereavement and to separation' (1999: 54). Fear of death is a universal human condition (Becker 2011). Human beings first acquire knowledge of death around the age of five, when they develop the requisite capacity for reflection and conceptual knowledge, of which other species appear to be incapable. Regardless of culture, ethnicity and religion, children gain an understanding of death as irreversible, final and inevitable (Papadatou 2015).

The other basic precondition for grief, in addition to an understanding of death, is the capacity to love. Again, it can be argued that humans possess a deeper capacity for love than other animals because our love relates to specific individuals. According to the Danish psychologist Jens Mammen, humans possess an extraordinary sense of the concrete (Mammen 1996; Mammen and Mironenko 2015). In other words, humans know that even if two objects are identical in every relevant respect, they are still two different, independent objects. For example, if I have two coins from 1975, and they are exactly the same down to the smallest detail, one of them can still have an emotional value that the other does not. If I was given one by my grandmother – as a memento of the year I was born – losing it would sadden me. It would be no consolation that I had another coin from that year, because it was not the one that my grandmother gave me. It was not the coin that had travelled through time and space from my grandmother's purse to my coin collection. We experience the world not just through our sensory perception of things as they appear on their surface (which Mammen calls sense categories), but also through our recognition of their historical depth. Objects do not just have qualitative, surface properties, they also have a *numerical identity*, in other words they are identical with themselves over time, and this makes them different from other single things that are qualitatively identical (in this case, Mammen talks of selection categories). The human senses are primed to recognise the numerical identity of things (i.e. their distinct identity), and this capacity is, of course, particularly important for our relationship to other people. While a loved one's qualitative characteristics change over time, as they grow older, and become more grey and wrinkled, they are still the same person in the numerical sense. Human love does not concern just the sum of the qualitative properties of the other, but the individual as an indivisible, unique whole. It may be assumed that animals cannot love in this way. If a dog's new owner is the identical twin of their old one, and looks (and smells) exactly the same in every way, the dog will presumably not notice the difference. Dogs do not possess the human sense of numerical particularity. They recognise the world via more superficial categories of senses.

What does this have to do with grief? Well, if love is a prerequisite for grief, and if this human sense of the concrete is a prerequisite for love, then our understanding of the other as a particular individual who is more than the sum of their attributes is, in fact, a prerequisite for the grief felt when the other is gone. The TV series *Black Mirror* presented a science-fiction scenario in which a woman grieving the loss of her husband was offered a copy of the deceased.[8]

At first, she is only offered the chance to text her deceased husband. In the show's vision of the future, everybody's digital activity – their messages, comments and searches – is stored in the cloud, and a supercomputer uses it to generate statements similar to those the deceased would have made in response to various questions (the technology is not particularly fanciful). Later, she gets to talk with him on the phone, as his voice has also been preserved. The story culminates with the bereaved widow receiving a physical copy of her dead husband, an android that is 100 per cent identical with him. It has the same look, the same voice, the same personality and the same habits. In one of the last scenes in the story, everything has gone wrong. The widow and the android are standing on a clifftop, and she, in her desperation, has ordered it to commit suicide. She has come to realise that the dead man cannot be replaced, even though the replacement is in almost all ways identical to the deceased. (In fact, the only difference is that the replacement is a slightly better lover.)

What she loved about her husband was not the sum of his attributes, but the man himself. Even if the replacement is a perfect copy, in which every molecule is identical, it is still just a copy. As she says to the android, 'You're just a few ripples of you. There's no history to you.' And it's true. The android may even have the subjective memories of the man's life and his history together with the woman, but it (or he?) has not travelled through time and space with the widow – and that makes all the difference. The man and the android are qualitatively identical, but numerically different. The object of grief is the loss of numerical particularity – not the loss of qualitative characteristics (which it will often be possible to replace with other ones, possibly even better ones). The story ends with the widow still incapable of destroying the android. She hides him in the attic and goes up there sometimes on her daughter's birthday, so that they can talk to the copy of the father for a while.

The episode of *Black Mirror* clearly illustrates what it might otherwise take a doctoral thesis to explain. It is notable that our sense of numerical identity and the concrete other is so deeply engrained in our relationships to other people (and to the world at large) that we must turn to science-fiction allegories in order to convey and analyse it. It is, quite simply, the essence of our being-in-the-world. It is grief as an emotion that reminds us of the uniqueness and irreplaceability of others. Ontologically, this means that there is something about loss that cannot be replaced. Bereaved individuals are often able, psychologically speaking, to find love – after a period of mourning, they may even regain their lust for life and love somebody else; but the loss itself is irreversible. The dead cannot be replaced, because every individual is unique. It is certainly possible to establish new relationships and love again, but they are exactly that: *new* relationships.

In this context, we need to distinguish between ontology and psychology. The loss of a child or spouse is not diminished in an ontological sense by a new child or a new spouse, even though it may, of course, be psychologically beneficial to establish relationships with others in the wake of a loss. The newer grief theories, i.e. those that focus on continuing bonds, have now recognised this (Klass, Silverman and Nickman 1996). From this perspective, the task of the bereaved is not to break their bonds with the deceased and 'move on', but to maintain those bonds and move through life 'together with' the deceased, who persist in the form of memories, stories and objects that frame the relationship (more about this in Chapter 5). The theory of 'continuous bonds' is meant descriptively, to illustrate how people actually grieve. However, it is also sometimes used normatively, as a model for 'natural' grief.

Ultimately, our ability to grieve is an expression of the human way of existing in the world, because it says something about our fundamental, existential relationship with love, death and the concrete other. This is not to romanticise grief, which of course can be relentlessly painful, and even psychologically debilitating. Rather, it is to emphasise that certain facts about humans are best understood through an emotion like grief, which is in this sense foundational. Perhaps precisely for that reason, very few people would want to live without grief when a loved one has died. What would a long life be without grief? It would by necessity be a life in which there is no acknowledgment of the reality of death, or a life without love (or perhaps without both). It would hardly be worth living. However, what if we could have grief without pain? Wouldn't that be great? Staying within the realms of science fiction, let us imagine that a pill is invented that removes the psychological pain of grief. We would still have the memories, but without the painful longing. We could browse photo albums containing pictures of a dead child, and it would only inspire smiles and happy thoughts. This may sound appealing on the surface, but my guess is that few of us would take such a pill. Why not? If a pill could eliminate pain and sadness, why would we not take it? The answer is probably that the pain of loss is an intrinsic part of grief – it is a love without a home. The pain is meaningful precisely because it reminds us of our continuing bonds to those we have lost. If grief is a foundational emotion, as this chapter has sought to argue, then to eliminate the pain of grief is to eliminate a fundamental aspect of our nature. Grief is the price of love, and our willingness to pay it is part of what makes us human.

Conclusions

This chapter's main concern has been to argue that grief should be considered a foundational emotion in the existential sense – on a par with anxiety, shame and guilt, which are otherwise often identified and discussed as such in existential philosophy, from Genesis to Nietzsche. I have suggested that the concept of foundational emotions reflects the aspect of our emotional life that is closely linked to our reflexive selfhood. In other words, these are the emotions that make us human. It is not just the ability to solve problems and other cognitive capacities that distinguishes us from other animals, but a certain sensitivity. *Homo sapiens* is, as it were, also *homo sentimentalis*. The chapter does not claim a linear, ontogenetic link between the development of this fundamental register of emotions and reflexive selfhood – although, empirically speaking, this may turn out to be the case – but rather that there is an existential link between grief, love, death and the human self. I have also argued that even though grief is immensely painful and difficult to endure, it orients us to the world in a way that we would not want to be without.

In addition, I have introduced and defended a version of the appraisal theories of emotions. These originated with Aristotle and are found today in cognitive, social-constructionist and phenomenological variants. They share as a point of departure the idea that emotions are epistemic, i.e. able to provide humans with knowledge and insights about the world. Emotions can be reasonable, and grief specifically can tell us something about the human being as a dependent, rational animal. Indeed, the philosopher Alasdair MacIntyre wrote a book titled *Dependent Rational Animals*, in which he combines classic Aristotelian virtue ethics with a modern biological understanding of human beings (MacIntyre 1999). Most of the Western philosophical and scientific canon has focused on the rational dimension of humanity (derived from Aristotle's conception of a *zoon logikon*), but our dependency on others and the emotions that express this dependency are just as important. The basic distinction between rationality and emotionality is problematic. Our foundational emotions (anxiety, shame, guilt and grief) can certainly be rational in situations where we recognise life's possibility (anxiety), the demands of community (shame), moral responsibility (guilt) and the irreversible loss of loved ones (grief). Foundational emotions are not irrational, but represent both affective and rational ways in which humans manifest their ability to understand and reflect on existence. I suspect that this is particularly evident in the case of grief, as it is as grieving animals that we are most directly aware of our nature as relational beings.

The foundational emotions listed in this chapter do not constitute an exhaustive list, but rather an invitation to explore how people become human not only through the development of purely rational faculties, but also through affective abilities and dispositions. Zinck and Newen (2008) have described a developmental trajectory for emotions throughout human life, from pre-emotions (diffuse affective states) to basic emotions, and finally to various kinds of cognitive emotions that require a complex, reflexive self – which is perhaps both a precondition for and a product of the reflexive emotions. A future research project ought to examine the ontogeny of the foundational emotions in greater depth.

In the next chapter, I present a more focused phenomenological description and discussion of grief.

3

The Phenomenology of Grief

Studies in psychology and related disciplines often begin with a particular model of the mind, which is then used to look at specific phenomena. Psychoanalysts, for example, operate with a certain understanding of the mind, and their studies seek to reveal unconscious processes through dreams, jokes or slips of the tongue. Classical behaviourists view the mind as a stimulus-response machine (referred to as a 'black box'), and that approach determines the nature of the experiments they conduct. Cognitivists try to open these 'black boxes' in laboratories and study how information is processed between stimuli and responses. The list goes on, and could include everything from theories of evolutionary psychology to those of narrative psychology.

I see nothing wrong with this approach per se, although there is often a risk of the theoretical outlook dictating the phenomena subsequently revealed. In other words, the theory determines the phenomenon. While this is problematic, it is preferable to a purely empiricist or positivist approach, which does not seek to make theory an essential part of scientific work.

Research in the field of psychology is often quite explicitly theory-driven, based on the hypothetico-deductive
method. This involves deducing a hypothesis from a
general theory and testing it on observable data, which
will ideally lead to an adjustment of the original theory.
However, a theoretical outlook often lurks somewhere
in the background, perhaps in the form of a basic scientific vocabulary. Scientists are generally unwilling
to abandon their theoretical perspectives, even when
confronted with seemingly contradictory observations.
If that happens, they often resort to blaming a faulty
experimental set-up ('keep the theory, discard the data').
Thomas Kuhn clearly described this in his classic work
on paradigms and scientific revolutions. According to
Kuhn (1970), the basic scientific paradigms usually
only change when influential representatives of the old
paradigm die. Even scientists are, quite simply, deeply
reluctant to admit that the theory on which they built
their whole career might actually be wrong.

In this chapter – based on the concept of grief as
a foundational emotion discussed in Chapter 2 – I
suggest a different way of thinking about the relationship between theories of the mind and psychological
phenomena. I do not propose just replacing the hypothetico-deductive model with an inductive one. This
has already been suggested by the positivists, with their
'verificationism' and distrust of theories (cf. Ayer 1990),
and by the 'grounded theorists' with their qualitative
studies (Glaser and Strauss 1967). I prefer to think that
significant research can emerge from both deductive and
inductive approaches – both by testing hypotheses and
by conducting more open experiments – but I also contend that the most direct route to valid theories of the

human mind is to begin with the question posed in Kantian transcendental philosophy: X exists – how is X possible? In psychology, a transcendental approach would look something like this: psychological phenomenon X exists – what, therefore, must the mind be like (i.e. what theory of the mind is needed) in order to account for the existence of X?

I hasten to add that I am not saying this in order to advocate Immanuel Kant's general transcendental theory of the mind, with its numerous a priori forms and categories as such (Kant 1998). This book has a far more phenomenological perspective than does Kant's a priori rationalism. On the other hand, I do think that Kant's transcendental question is generally helpful and should be posed more often. We experience something – what made it possible? This question seeks to discover how a phenomenon that actually exists, *can* exist. Transcendental questions are generally about the conditions of possibility for something or other, and the answers to these questions require a very careful phenomenology specific to the X in question. It is vital that X (the phenomenon) is adequately understood and described if it is to act as a foundation in the formulation of a more general theory of mind that explains how X is possible. The general thrust of this strategy is clear: it is about starting with fully developed psychological phenomena in their holistic forms and then working toward a theory of mind that respects the essential features of these phenomena and accounts for how they arise. The aim is to start with the higher psychological functions (for example, how people reason, make complex choices and have reflexive emotions such as shame and grief) and then construct a non-reductive theoretical account of them (Valsiner et al. 2016).

As mentioned previously, this book emerged out of 'The Culture of Grief' research project, part of which looks at the ongoing transformations in the ways people experience grief today. At the start of the project, we were immediately confronted with a number of difficult questions: what is grief? Is it a universal human phenomenon? What is its function? How has it developed throughout history? How much does grief vary between cultures? How much does it vary between individuals? Is it ever legitimate to consider grief a mental disorder? All of these questions are discussed at various points in this book. I only mention them now to illustrate how different answers to these questions follow quite logically from different pre-established theories of the mind. For example, evolutionary psychological theories will lead down one path (see, e.g. Archer 1999), cultural-psychological and anthropological theories another (see, e.g. Scheper-Hughes 1993). It appears to me that scholars (not necessarily the ones cited here) often have an entrenched theory of the mind and simply apply it to grief, a tendency that makes it very difficult to identify new and surprising insights not already predicted by the theory. This is particularly true when it comes to grief interventions in practice – an extremely broad field that has often been approached in a fairly narrow way, according to a specific theoretical understanding (for example, psychoanalysis or attachment theory). In this chapter, I therefore pose the following Kantian questions: grief exists as a phenomenon – what general psychological theory of mind do we need to account for its possibility? How does the human mind have to be constituted to allow for the possibility of grief? In a sense, this chapter uses grief as a key to unlock the human mind, which is a natural follow-up to the previous chapter's account of grief as a foundational emotion for the human self.

The chapter starts with a phenomenological description of grief. This is central to the book's overall project, and serves to define some important properties of grief. I then discuss three general psychological implications of the existence of grief: (1) the deep relationality of the self, (2) the limitations of evolutionary accounts in psychology, and (3) the normativity of psychological phenomena. While I would argue that these are general psychological insights arising from the phenomenon of grief, it is fair to say that they could equally be reached via studies of other important psychological phenomena. Naturally, there are many more implications than just the three presented here, but I believe that these are the ones that are of the greatest general value to psychology and the humanities.

Identifying the phenomenology of grief

As mentioned previously, phenomenology seeks to reveal the human experience from a first-person perspective. A few scholars in recent years have tried to describe grief from a phenomenological perspective. Fuchs, for example, adopts a phenomenological approach in his attempt to map the 'core structure to the experience of grief' (2018: 45). He concludes that grief has interpersonal, temporal and bodily aspects. He describes it as an emotion that comes after the initial shock and numbness following a bereavement: 'Often the bereaved person closes his eyes or throws his hands before his face in despair, as if to stop vision. This is accompanied by a general bodily exhaustion, passivity, and lack of drive which severely restrict one's initiative and scope of action. Finally, loss of appetite and sleep disturbances also resemble the symptoms of depression' (2018: 46). Fuchs mentions depression because one of the goals of his study is to arrive at a valid distinction between it and grief. He uses the popular amputation metaphor – grief is often described as being akin to losing a limb. According to Fuchs, the most important experiential features of grief are a sense of heaviness in the body, passivity, constriction and withdrawal (2018: 46). However, the characteristic bodily signs of depression, such as rigidity and loss of affective resonance (the ability to be emotionally moved), are not part of grief. When a person loses someone close – perhaps a life-long partner – they experience a rupture of what Fuchs calls intercorporeality: 'The threads of mutual attachment and belonging are cut off, and the wound or pain that is now felt bears resemblance to an amputation of the "dyadic body" that one has formed with the other' (2018: 47). Fuchs also addresses the temporality of grief and emphasises the commonly reported sensation of time standing still after a bereavement: 'the future is no longer experienced as an open horizon of possibilities and projects' (2018: 51).

In a similar vein, Ratcliffe argues that a core element of the phenomenology of grief lies in the loss of 'systems of opportunity' in relation to the dead person (2017: 4). When we lose a loved one, we also lose the whole interpersonal system of relating to the other, which otherwise operated as a backdrop to life and endowed it with meaning. The ways in which we spoke together, interacted with each other, touched each other, slept together, loved each other, etc., are all gone. This confirms a key point emphasised by Attig, that grief is a process in which we have to 'relearn' the world. In other words, it involves constructing a new system of possibilities, part of which involves maintaining bonds with the deceased. In line with Heidegger's existential phenomenology, Attig defines the self as 'a network of caring connections' (2004: 348). The phenomenological analyses presented here illustrate that this network is deeply anchored in the body of the bereaved, and functions as a system of possibilities for action and meaning in relation to significant others. I will return to this notion of the grieving body in Chapter 4.

In applying a phenomenological approach, Fuchs and Ratcliffe have, in my opinion, identified some key features of grief, particularly in terms of how it is generally experienced, its rupture of intercorporeality, how it affects our experience of time, and first and foremost the loss of a system of possibilities. While I believe that these descriptions have general validity, I would like to point out an omission – one that is fundamental, yet easily overlooked – namely, that grief by necessity involves *the loss of another* in an ontological sense. In my view, Fuchs and Ratcliffe place too great an emphasis on *the loss of possibilities* in a purely psychological sense, as if the other – the loved one who has died – only existed for the sake of the bereaved. I believe that an adequate phenomenology of grief must begin with an understanding of loss as an ontological reality. In his famous and remarkably candid memoir *A Grief Observed*, C.S. Lewis expresses a similar thought (not, of course, in response to Fuchs and Ratcliffe, but as a reaction to his own loss). After describing the phenomenology of grief, for example by likening it to the experience of anxiety (butterflies in the stomach, restlessness), Lewis reflects critically on his own account: 'For the first time I have looked back and read these notes. They appal me. From the way I've been talking anyone would think that H's death mattered chiefly for its effect on myself. Her point of view seems to have dropped out of sight' (1961: 16). Later, Lewis confirms that he is mourning his wife (whom he refers to as H) as an independent person, in all of her uniqueness (see the previous chapter about the human sense of the concrete), and not simply what she represented *for him*:

> All reality is iconoclastic. The earthly beloved, even in this life, incessantly triumphs over your mere idea of her. And you want her to; you want her with all her resistances, all her faults, all her unexpectedness. That is, in her foursquare and independent reality. And this, not any image or memory, is what we are to love still, after she is dead. (1961: 56)

This idea is quite simple, but somewhat difficult to express phenomenologically using Fuchs and Ratcliffe's approaches. They base their writings on Husserl's original phenomenology, which is a strict, descriptive science about the structures of experience. However, it also has certain weaknesses, in particular in its tendency to 'reduce the other to the same', as Emmanuel Levinas (1969) famously argued in his critique of Husserl. Levinas's post-Husserlian phenomenology was an attempt to respect *the otherness of the other* as an essential aspect of our experience, instead of making

71

the other into something that has meaning only in relation to us. In Davis's book on Levinas, he spells out the
problem that he (Levinas) saw in Husserl's phenomenology: 'consciousness can never meet anything truly
alien to itself because the external world is a product of
its own activity' (Davis 1996: 19). Writing more positively about Levinas's contribution, Davis states that
what is at stake in his discussions of intentionality 'is
the ability of consciousness to encounter something
other than itself. If meaning is entirely given by the subject rather than found in the world, then consciousness
cannot experience, perceive or learn anything that it did
not already contain' (1996: 19). Levinas was working
toward a conception of subjectivity as 'radically turned
outwards, maintaining an openness to the non-self
which is not subsumed under the categories of representation or knowledge' (1996: 20). He would probably
agree with C.S. Lewis that 'all reality is iconoclastic'.
The other is more than my image (icon, representation)
of them, which pales beside the reality. The people in
our lives do not exist merely as the mental representations of them in our minds, but as real people with their
own lives and stories, which are far broader than we can
possibly comprehend. We must not, therefore, reduce
the other to our representations of them – including in
their absence after death. The reality of the other simply
surpasses any image we may form of them. This was
also the theme of the episode of *Black Mirror* discussed
in the previous chapter, where the widow was offered
a copy, a representation, of her dead husband. This, in
a nutshell, is Levinas's great contribution to phenomenology. It is noteworthy that the subtitle to his grand
work *Totality and Infinity* is *An Essay on Exteriority*.

Husserlian phenomenology takes insufficient account of the other's exteriority or radical otherness.

This does not alter the fact that Fuchs's and Ratcliffe's concrete phenomenological descriptions are both valid and precise. Rather, it adds to them an important point about grief as a response to the death of the other. Grief is not just about my own lost possibilities and future plans with the bereaved, no matter how important they might be. Grief is not just about the fact that *I* lose someone, purely psychologically. It is also about the more fundamental fact that *someone no longer exists*. It might be said that I do not grieve my loss, as if the death of the other were reducible to my subjective response to their death. I do not mourn only the loss of a system of possibility. I also grieve the fundamental fact that the other has passed away. This also explains why we may grieve the loss of people we did not know personally and who did not exist for us as a 'system of possibilities' (Lady Diana, Prince, David Bowie et al.). There is very little intercorporeality between such famous figures and ordinary people, and yet many of us nonetheless experience quite profound grief when we learn that our idols have passed away.

The human capacity for knowing that the other exists in their particular otherness – and not only in their meaning for oneself – is related to what Mammen calls the human 'sense of the concrete' (see previous chapter). That is to say, the other person whom we love is not just a collection of qualitative characteristics that we perceive with the senses ('sense categories'), but is also a person with numerical identity, which we understand through 'choice categories'. We grieve when the numerical identity of the other has gone, and they now only exist in the form of memories. The next section looks at three of the general psychological implications of grief.

The deep relationality of the self

Now that we have used Husserlian and Levinasian insights to outline the contours of a phenomenology of grief, it is time to explore how this informs theoretical work on understanding the human mind. First of all, I believe that it teaches us something about the deep relationality of the self. By this, I mean that the individual is not a socially atomised being who can choose to connect with others or not. We cannot be 'internalists' about the human self, in the sense that knowledge about the individual is in itself sufficient to understand the person. Rather, we need to be 'relationalists', and acknowledge that the self exists only in terms of its networks of relationships. The individual only exists because they interact with others, who see, recognise and forge bonds with them. We encountered this idea earlier, in the form of Kierkegaard's famous analysis of the self as a relationship that relates to itself, but which is determined by something else. For Kierkegaard, this 'something else' is, ultimately, God. However, in the context of secular social psychology, such as the early twentieth-century work of George Herbert Mead, it is others in society who determine the self. For Mead, being self-aware – having a self – is not simply the ability to look inward and observe an inner object (the self). It involves the ability to relate to oneself through other people's reactions and perspectives, and for this reason communication is central to self-consciousness.

The Phenomenology of Grief

'The individual experiences himself as such, not directly, but only indirectly, . . . "communication" . . . provides a form of behaviour in which the organism or the individual may become an object to himself' (Mead 2015: 138). In his famous book *Mind, Self and Society*, from which this quote is taken, Mead shows how human beings emerge by learning to relate reflexively to themselves, supported by relationships to others.

This book draws on Mead's relational-reflexive perspective, but has a different emphasis – namely, on the importance of emotional life for the reflexive self (see the previous chapter on grief as a foundational emotion). Both the self and society are in a sense constituted by the human ability to experience deep existential emotions such as grief, which express a connection both to the concrete other and to a larger social community that reproduces itself across generations. It is again worth quoting Attig at this juncture. He argues that grief reveals that the (Western) idea of the self as a 'self-contained social atom' is totally misguided. We therefore need other metaphors to understand ourselves. He suggests viewing the self 'as a web of caring connections to elements in the world around us. This self, in turn, is enmeshed within a web of webs encompassing our families and communities' (2004: 348). This echoes the famous closing words of Merleau-Ponty's magnum opus *Phenomenology of Perception*, which quotes de Saint-Exupéry: 'Man is but a network of relationships, and these alone matter to him' (Merleau-Ponty 2012: 530). Løgstrup would call this network of relationships the *interdependence* in human existence.

This approach to the self or the person in Western

75

thought is by no means obvious. From an anthropological viewpoint, Clifford Geertz observed that:

> The Western conception of the person as a bounded, unique, more or less integrated motivational and cognitive universe, a dynamic center of awareness, emotion, judgment, and action organized into a distinctive whole and set contrastively both against other such wholes and against its social and natural background, is, however incorrigible it may seem to us, a rather peculiar idea within the context of the world's cultures. (1983: 59)

The philosopher Charles Taylor argued that the Western idea of the self as an inner realm of thoughts and feelings, which he traces and discusses throughout his opus *Sources of the Self*, is 'a function of a historically limited mode of self-interpretation, one which has become dominant in the modern West and which may indeed spread thence to other parts of the globe, but which had a beginning in time and space and may have an end' (1989: 111).

While Geertz and Taylor's insights are incredibly valuable, the point of this chapter is that these conclusions can be arrived at not just by discussing the historical and cultural origins of the idea of the self, but also (more directly) through a meticulous phenomenology of grief. As Ratcliffe puts it: 'Studying the phenomenology of grief thus serves to illustrate the – often insufficiently acknowledged – extent to which the experienced world, our sense of rootedness within it and our ability to act in meaningful ways all depend upon other people' (2017: 16). The human capacity to grieve shows us that our selves are deeply interconnected – they are permeable and open. This is in contrast to the sealed-off, closed selves of much of Western thought, in which the individual is considered almost as an elementary, isolated particle. We saw above how Davis described Levinas's view of the subject as 'radically turned outwards' in relation to others. Fuchs explains: 'Like hardly any other psychic phenomenon, grief discloses the fact that as human beings we are fundamentally related to, and in need of others, that indeed our self is permeable and open to them.' He continues: 'This expansion and mutual overlap of selves may be regarded as the most essential presupposition of grief. [. . .] This renders me fundamentally vulnerable, for in losing the other, I lose 'half of my self', as it were' (2018: 48, 49).

Losing something of oneself is arguably the most prevalent metaphor in people's accounts of grief. If the analysis presented above is correct, we should actually take this metaphor quite literally. In a major study of reactions to grief, based on an online questionnaire, 27 per cent of the more than 7,000 respondents reported that they '*never* went back to feeling like themselves after their loss' (Granek 2013: 282). When we lose a loved one, in a way we lose part of ourselves, in the sense that the self is constituted by relationships with others. This is a key finding in phenomenological studies of grief: that bereavement severs the habitually constituted intercorporeality between persons that represents a significant aspect of the human self. This leads to a feeling of psychological amputation or loss of self. In his memoir, C.S. Lewis described it as follows: 'I think I am beginning to understand why grief feels like suspense. It comes from the frustration of so many impulses that had become habitual. Thought after thought, feeling after feeling, action after action, had H. for their object. Now their target is gone' (1961: 41). The 'target' is gone, but the impulses persist, like the sensation of a phantom limb.

I have argued here that an in-depth phenomenology of grief will, in principle, falsify those theories that understand the self in atomistic terms, as bounded and closed. The point is not to explicate these (falsified) theories, nor to articulate better ones that actually do respect the deep relationality of the self. That being said, we may be better served by Taylor's view of the self as arising within 'webs of interlocution' (1989: 36), or MacIntyre's (1999) definition of human beings as 'dependent rational animals'. A valid understanding of grief equips us with certain arguments that necessitate a relational idea of the self (which may take many forms) and excludes others that are non-relational. To truly understand grief as a phenomenon is to rule out psychological 'internalism' (the idea that it is possible to understand the individual in isolation from others).

The limitations of evolutionary theories

The evolutionary perspective on psychological phenomena has become very widespread – not just in sociobiology and evolutionary psychology, but also much more broadly. It would be a brave soul indeed who questioned the evolutionary origin of *Homo sapiens* and of the conscious mind, and I have no intention of doing so here. Modern psychology is unthinkable without a background in evolutionary thinking. To my mind, this is how it should be, since any account of psychological phenomena must be able to explain the emergence of the mind in both its natural and cultural-historical forms. The question, then, is to what extent we can reach conclusions about the human mind *directly* from an evolutionary framework, and whether we can ever separate what has evolved naturally from what has been acquired culturally. The evolutionary framework has a tendency to approach psychological phenomena by evaluating their adaptive value, which leads to quite narrow questions about utility, and in this light grief is particularly challenging. In simple terms, evolutionary accounts claim that our psychological functions exist because they had survival value in the past, often based on rather speculative accounts of life on the savannahs of East Africa around 100,000 years ago.

What, then, does evolutionary psychology make of the phenomenon of grief? A classic authoritative source on this approach is 'Evolutionary Psychology: A Primer' by leading scholars Leda Cosmides and John Tooby, a programmatic text on the website of the Center for Evolutionary Psychology. The authors describe evolutionary psychology in an admirably clear manner by outlining what they see as its five fundamental principles. They emphasise that it is not a special area of study in psychology (like vision or cognition), but an *approach* to psychology as a whole. They define psychology as 'that branch of biology that studies (1) brains, (2) how brains process information, and (3) how the brain's information-processing programs generate behavior'. The fundamental principles of evolutionary psychology include the following: 'Our neural circuits were designed by natural selection to solve problems that our ancestors faced during our species' evolutionary history' (Principle 2); 'Different neural circuits are specialized for solving different adaptive problems' (Principle 4);

and the summative belief that 'Our modern skulls house a Stone Age mind' (Principle 5).

Sometimes the theory is likened to a Swiss Army knife, in that the human mind has a number of different functions that solve different existential tasks, which must have been related to reproduction and survival early in our evolutionary history. The theory is often coupled with the modular approach found in cognitive neuroscience, which conceives of the mind as an array of separate functions or 'modules'. In the case of grief, however, it is very difficult to account for it within a modular and evolutionary framework. What would be the adaptive value of the kind of 'non-functional' behaviour associated with bereavement? When grieving, a person often ceases to engage in their normal day-to-day activities such as production and reproduction, which seems to counteract the evolutionary account. This explains why most grief scholars, who otherwise subscribe to some form of evolutionary psychology, see grief as a *by-product* of something else that can be understood in terms of survival value (Archer 1999). Archer points to John Bowlby, who proposed that the evolutionary purpose of grief – as a kind of separation anxiety – is that it motivates the individual to seek reunion (1999: 5). Similarly, Colin Murray Parkes views grief as 'a consequence of the way we form personal relationships'. Thus, Archer concludes, grief is, in an evolutionary perspective, 'the cost we pay for being able to love in the way we do' (1999: 5). It is a by-product of the relationships we form as a social species. Later, Archer even says that 'grief itself is maladaptive, but is connected to features which are adaptive' (1999: 159). In other words, it emerges from human relationality.

This is probably the best possible account of grief from an evolutionary perspective. However, in my opinion, it should lead us to seriously question the universal explanatory value of the theory of evolution within psychology. If there is no adaptive 'grief module', and if grief in itself is maladaptive, then not only the emotion of grief as such, but the many cultural customs and practices that surround it appear almost incomprehensible.

Sociologists such as Emile Durkheim and Peter Berger have emphasised the important social and cultural significance of grief. Durkheim argued that the manner in which bereaved people integrate the dead into their own lives 'is central to how society itself perpetuates itself, for if the dead are not integrated then society disconnects from its own past and ultimately from itself' (Walter 1999: 20). Berger said that every human society ultimately amounts to little more than 'men banded together in the face of death' (Berger quoted by Walter 1999: 21). Humans have built pyramids and memorials, written testaments, constructed shrines and cemeteries and collected memorabilia in order to integrate the dead into the life of the living, and connect the past, present and future. As mentioned earlier, Granek describes grief as a thread 'that moves across societies, institutions, communities, and relationships' and binds relationships over time (2013: 283).

The point of all this is to say that if a defining characteristic of *Homo sapiens* – our capacity for grief – is not well understood within an evolutionary framework, then this should perhaps lead us to doubt whether evolutionary psychology and related perspectives really deserve the attention they currently receive as universal theories of the human mind. Again, I must stress that I do not deny the general importance of our evolutionary past. However, there is probably no direct route from this past to an understanding of the psychological and existential realities that exist for individuals in our current cultural contexts. What the evolutionary perspective lacks in particular is an understanding of the socio-cultural normativity of psychological phenomena such as grief, which brings us to the third lesson to be learned from grief as a human phenomenon.

The normativity of psychological phenomena

Although psychology often claims to be a causal science seeking to reveal laws of human behaviour, there is good reason to believe that psychological phenomena are more normative than causal. This is because humans should be understood as actors who *perform* or *do* their actions, thoughts and emotions – these cannot be understood as just something that simply happens to them. As seen in the previous chapter, this perspective stretches all the way back to Aristotle. I defined anger and grief as psychological phenomena, whereas fatigue and constipation are physiological. The former are situated within a normative moral order, where individuals, at least once they are adults, are held responsible for their emotions. Aristotle did not deny that emotions have a physiological component (he thought, for example, that anger was accompanied by a boiling of the blood), but physiology is just one aspect of emotional life. The second – and more important – aspect consists of the 'dialectical' or normative, in which anger is a response to injustice, just as grief is a normative response to the loss of a loved one. Anger and grief are psychological phenomena in so far as they are normative phenomena that can be 'done' more or less well, and are things for which individuals may be praised or blamed. If anger and grief were purely causal reactions, they would belong to the realm of physiology (not psychology), and it would be unreasonable to hold people accountable for their emotions.

It is obvious that certain psychological processes are 'carried out'. For example, when someone tries to perform mathematical calculations, we cannot meaningfully say that this 'happens' to them. But most of our emotional life lies in a grey area between what *happens* and what is *done*. After a bereavement, we might feel that our grief is overwhelming – it is like floating in the sea and being hit by a big wave. We are overwhelmed by sadness, and think of ourselves as victims of our emotions. But even this kind of emotion is not simply a mechanical reaction that happens to us, the inevitable result of cause and effect. Grief is also *performed* by human actors, who can only *grieve properly* if they are aware of the dominant moral order in which they are situated (Harré 1983), the social practices which tell them *how* to grieve and *how much* grief is required (Kofod and Brinkmann 2017). Grief is not simply a mechanical *reaction*, but rather a *response* to a loss; and the loss is not simply a *cause* that mechanically triggers an emotion, but an *invitation* to the bereaved to feel and express certain emotions. This is perhaps easiest to understand if we look at how children learn to feel grief. Interestingly, it is clear that they learn a specific, normatively preferred form of response.

Below is a real account of an early memory of loss

and grief, that was written and sent to me by somebody I know. This is, of course, just one single, illustrative description, but I nonetheless believe that it conveys some general truths about the normativity of grief. The person in question is a Chilean woman in her thirties, who now lives in Denmark:

This short story is about one of my first encounters with grief. These memories came to me as I reflected on how we are socialised to grieve during childhood. So it is likely that the way I tell the story is shaped by my background as a cultural psychologist and my specific interest in learning and childhood.

First, I should mention a couple of things regarding the context for my memories. I was born and grew up in Calama, a rough mining town in the middle of the desert in the north of Chile. My childhood was during the last decade of the dictatorship in Chile and the first decade of the transition to democracy. This story took place when I was 12. Before then, I have no clear memories of having participated in funerals or experiencing the death of someone close. Not even pets. My grandfather died when I was three years old, and I only have some vague snapshots of my mother crying, and the mood in the home changing. My grandfather lived with us, and people say that he and I were close.

In 1992, I had started seventh grade at a new private school, and I was one of the oldest children there. It was a small school with just over 80 pupils. It was more like a big family than an anonymous institution. Everybody knew everybody in some way or another. In the teachers' eyes, I was a good student, so I was chosen to sit on the student council. Toward the end of the first year, the father of one of my fellow pupils died. He had founded the new school. I do not remember the cause of death, but my impression is that it was sudden. The school management decided that the student council members should attend the funeral on behalf of the other students. I remember thinking that I had barely talked to this boy, who was a year younger than me, and that I did not know his parents. I remember feeling sorry for him, but apprehensive about the situation. It is strange that I only remember the boy because he actually also had a little sister. Maybe I just thought that he was closer to my group of friends than his sister was, and so my attention was directed toward him.

As I said before, I had never attended a funeral, so I did not know what to do or say, or what was expected of me. I remember being anxious that my uniform and hair looked clean and nice. I was sitting with a straight back, I was quiet and avoided talking to the others. I tried to follow those who seemed to know more than I did. To my relief, I at least knew some of the Catholic traditions, so I could follow the service. My parents were not particularly religious, and I remember feeling ashamed and guilty about not knowing the church's protocols every time I went to a service. I even asked them several times, without success, if we could go to church on Sundays.

I cannot remember exactly whether the funeral was in a church or a chapel, but there was a service, and everything was decorated with colourful carnations, gladioli and some chrysanthemums. Rarely had I seen so many flowers, with so many colours. It was beautiful, but everyone was so sad. Even today, these flowers are to me flowers of death, and they belong at funerals and cemeteries.

I remember feeling that it was not enough to merely be the 'good student', and that I should do more. One by one, people went up to commiserate. Many cried and were clearly upset. I still have an image in my head of

85

the mother crying inconsolably, and the children by her side with sad faces. I really did not know what to say, so I started to listen to what the others said: 'Sorry for your loss', 'May God be with you', and I remember nervously trying to learn these phrases. Everybody seemed to be affected, and it was clearly a tragedy for the dead person and the family left behind. As well as feeling incompetent, I also felt extremely guilty about not being emotionally affected. But I simply did not know these people, and it was a new situation for me.

These emotions were mixed with fear. After expressing their condolences, most people approached the coffin, one end of which was open. Many said a few words directly to the dead man. I had never seen a dead person before, and I felt out of my depth, but I was fascinated. To my relief, the glass over the torso prevented you from seeing the dead man clearly. I felt guilty that I could not cry like the others. So I began to imagine scenarios in which people I loved were dead. What if my father did not come back from one of his business trips? What if grandma died? What if I never saw them again? As the tears began to fall, I felt relief that I had somehow made contact, and that I was able to express what I ought to express.

Although the details of the story above are specific to the individual concerned, many of us have similar childhood memories of the difficulty of finding and expressing the right sentiments following a death. This can be explained by the thesis of the normativity of grief. As with other emotions, we must learn the often implicit rules of how grief is supposed to be expressed in different situations. In the example, the girl was under normative pressure to be sad in the right way. An entire emotional drama played out, driven by guilt over not being able to feel proper grief and fear of doing something wrong. As an accomplished 'method actor', however, the girl managed to adapt to the situation by imagining that it was one of her own relations who had died, and this unleashed the tears she thought were required. It is worth noting that no one had given her explicit instructions for how people are supposed to behave. Normative expectations are much more subtle, and embedded in the situation. On the one hand, it might be said that there is something false about expressing grief when, as in this case, we are not really sad because we only had a peripheral relationship to the deceased. On the other hand, it is also a way of socialising children emotionally and incorporating them into the prevalent moral order.

In the situation of a funeral or other ceremony following a death, there is often, but not always, a quite clear normative choreography for displays of emotion. Studying parents who have lost an infant child, Kofod (2015) found that they struggle not only with the loss in itself, but also with navigating the rather unclear normativity surrounding this tragic situation. One prevailing cultural discourse asserts that the worst thing a human being can experience is the loss of a child. However, other discourse implies (to put it bluntly) that the loss is supposed to be less intense when a child dies very early (Kofod's participants lost their children either before, during or soon after giving birth), as opposed to older children that the parents 'have gotten to know'. So how – and how much – are parents supposed to grieve? This is not an easy question to answer, but the fact that Kofod's participants reflect upon it in conversations with the researcher lends support to the idea that the difficult emotions that overwhelm us also have a normative aspect. In other words, we do not just grieve formlessly out of nothing. It has to be done *correctly*, even if what is considered 'correct' is extremely wide and varied.

Summing up the normative aspect of grief, we find ourselves hurtling toward the same conclusion that Aristotle articulated in his 'hybrid psychology' (a theory of the mind as a state between physiology and normativity) a couple of millennia ago. He believed that psychological phenomena such as grief are normative and should be assessed in relation to standards and norms. In relation to this book's starting point, it is worth adding that this conclusion was also drawn by Husserl in his phenomenology (which was not specifically concerned with grief, but with human experience in general). Much of Husserl's work consisted of critiques of *psychologism*, which is the theory that logic and normativity can, in general terms, be explained with reference to how humans actually think and reason psychologically – in other words, that logic is based on psychology. Husserl rejected this, because it would mean reducing the normativity of logic to causal explanations of psychological systems. More generally, Husserl's phenomenology incorporated an awareness of the normativity of our experiences. He is perhaps best known for emphasising the intentionality of consciousness – that experiences are always *about* something. However, as Crowell puts it in his account of Husserl's phenomenology, 'intentionality is not simply the static presence of a "presentation" in a mental experience (*Erlebnis*) but a normatively oriented *claim to validity*' (2009: 13). Simply put, this means that what we experience (e.g. grief) can only intentionally be 'about' something (e.g. a loss) because there are more and less correct and valid ways of experiencing it (normatively). We experience normativity and values in objects and events – a position explored by the Gestalt psychologists in greater detail after Husserl (e.g. Köhler 1959). We do not experience a value-neutral world upon which we project meaning and value. Rather, meaning and value are the basis of our experience of the world. *Intentionality* (that our experience is directed toward something) and *normativity* (that there are more or less correct ways to experience something) are in this sense intimately linked. This idea is central to this book's phenomenological theory of emotional life in general, and of grief in particular.

Conclusions

In this chapter, I have argued that a fruitful way of building theories of mind and mental life is to begin with Kant's transcendental question: X exists – how is that possible? Grief exists – so what must a theory of mental life look like in order to account for this fact? I began with a phenomenology of grief, building on a combination of insights from both Husserl and Levinas. From the Husserlian perspective, we saw that grief is anchored in the body of the bereaved, as the loss of a system of possibilities. The Levinasian perspective revealed an insistence on focusing on the deceased other *as* other (and not just as reducible to my representation of the other). This perspective emphasises that grief is also an ontological event, at the centre of which is the person who has died. According to Levinas, we must distrust the otherwise dominant representational theories of the mind and insist on being iconoclasts (to use C.S. Lewis's word). In simple terms, we grieve the other's death. Our grief is directed at that. Not only at our *image* of the other.

From here, I tried to deduce three principles or tenets of psychology. First, that grief teaches us that any theory of mental life must acknowledge the deep relationality of the self; second, that evolutionary accounts focused on the adaptive value of psychological functions and experiences are severely limited in terms of their ability to explain existential phenomena such as grief; and third, that mental life and its phenomena are normative in the sense that they do not just happen (as mechanical reactions), but are lived and enacted in a normative, responsive space. I have argued elsewhere that this space is constituted by socio-cultural practices on which cultural psychologists and other students of the human mind should focus (Brinkmann 2006b; 2016b).

In this chapter, I sought to achieve three things: (1) to demonstrate the value of a phenomenological approach (starting with the Kantian question) to the development of theories about the human mind; (2) to establish a phenomenology of grief that embraces Levinas's significant correction of the theories arising from Husserl's work; and (3) to develop the initial contours of a general psychology of the mind and human emotions that is relational (albeit without abandoning the idea of the human as a being who experiences things), which pays attention to the human evolutionary past (albeit without seeing the whole of psychology in the light of evolutionary history), and that recognises the normative nature of mental life (albeit without this leading to a voluntarism according to which individuals simply choose their mental states, which would be absurd). Acknowledging grief's role as a basic existential phenomenon allows us to say something important about both the human self (see the previous chapter) and the psychological domain (this chapter). In the next chapter, I go on to discuss the role of the body in grief.

4

The Body in Grief –
Grief in the Body

Much of the literature on grief and bereavement over-
looks the role of the body.[9] Indeed, the term 'body' rarely
appears in the indexes of any of the key textbooks on
the subject. This is strange, given the significant physical
sensations involved and the archetypal representations
of grief in images of the human body. Most art muse-
ums, for example, feature visual representations of grief
(I discuss some examples below), and a simple Google
image search on the word 'grief' reveals striking similarities between the many hits. There are a few pictures
of eyes filled with tears, but the majority of the images
depict a human body bent forward, head bowed, and
with one or both hands supporting the head or covering the face – either the whole face or parts of it, such
as the eyes, mouth or forehead. The grieving person's
hands – and sometimes also their arms – are usually at
the centre of such images (either holding the head or
concealing the face), indicating that grief is conveyed
not only through facial expressions, but through the
whole body. Although grief is both felt and expressed
via the body, it would appear that the general absence

of the body in the literature on grief reflects the more widespread neglect of the body in Western psychology in general and emotion theory in particular, a matter to which I return below.

A standard definition of grief is that it is a 'reaction to bereavement, involving both psychological and bodily experiences' (Gross 2016: 5). Often, however, researchers and practitioners in thanatology (the scientific study of death and loss) ignore the bodily aspects. Another definition states that grief refers to 'the emotions that accompany bereavement', whereas mourning is 'the behaviour that social groups expect following bereavement' (Walter 1999: xv). In order to understand the role of the body in grief, it is important to have a solid theory of emotions, which I began to outline in the previous chapter and expand upon here. In recent years, research into emotion has grown exponentially, and has spread to disciplines such as psychology, sociology, biology, neuroscience and anthropology. Nonetheless, it seems reasonable to conclude that the body is rarely depicted as directly involved in emotional processes, and is at best portrayed as playing a more indirect role. In other words, it functions as a physiological organism that is observed and interpreted by the person, as in William James's classic theories of emotion (to which I also return later).

This chapter focuses directly on the otherwise neglected relationship between grief and the body, and argues that the body should be considered as a subject in this context. The person who grieves should always be understood as an incarnate (i.e. embodied) subject. As an emotion, grief is not an internal mental phenomenon, but a manifest, embodied process. We do not realise that we are in a state of grief by observing our bodies (as propounded in James 1983), rather we *are* our bodies in responsive processes of grief. Grief inscribes itself on the body, in a process that I refer to as *impression* – but it is also *expressed* by the body in various social and material contexts. In other words, on the one hand grief is a *cognitive* emotion that informs the grieving individual about something in the world; on the other hand, it is a *communicative* emotion that conveys significant information to others. Although this perspective, with its emphasis on observable behaviour, might sound close to behaviourism, like Ludwig Wittgenstein (1958) I reject this classification, because the body is not simply an element in a mechanical chain of causes and effects (loss and reaction). It is a responsive, experiencing, socialised body (Seale 1998). The body is what phenomenologists refer to as 'the lived body'. Grief is not something passive that simply *happens* to the body – it is *done* or *enacted* by the bereaved, embodied individual. My view – that grieving is both an emotional *reaction* (impression) and an active *response* (expression) – is shared by other significant approaches to grief, such as Attig's (2004) existential-phenomenological theory. However, in this chapter, I argue that not enough attention has been paid to the body's role in this process. I discuss the grieving body by drawing on science, the arts and theories of emotion in an attempt to refine a theory that will help us understand the bodily dynamics of grief.

The grieving body

In contemporary grief theory, the body is usually addressed in one of two ways. On the one hand, a substantial number of writers look at grief as a risk factor in somatic health. Popular culture is full of narratives on and studies of 'how grief weakens the body'[10] (often with a focus on 'broken heart syndrome'), and how grief allegedly makes us vulnerable to diseases such as the common cold, sore throats, infection, rheumatoid arthritis, asthma, cardiovascular disease and cancer.[11] There is also a body of literature on how different physical practices can help heal the grieving body, as well as a receptive market for therapeutic interventions of this type. Mary-Frances O'Connor (2013) has summarised much of the research on the physiological mechanisms involved in complicated grief, research which appears to position the body as a dependent variable, causally affected by grief. In other words, the body is conceived of as a variable rather than a living, experiencing, grieving body, which is the focus of this chapter. I have no intention of criticising the physiological or health-oriented perspective as such, but I would prefer to emphasise a phenomenological perspective on the body in grief.

On the other hand, a (much smaller) number of scholars have addressed the embodied experience of grief. Whereas the first approach looks at the body from physiological and medical perspectives, the second adopts a phenomenological approach. In a short article, J. Todd DuBose examines grief specifically from the perspective of a phenomenology of the body, based on the work of Merleau-Ponty. He describes the body as 'a relational matrix' that connects bereavement, grief and mourning (DuBose 1997: p. 369). In her qualitative study of the grieving body, one of very few to have been conducted, Maria Guðmundsdóttir (2009) adopted an existential phenomenology perspective. The study consisted of interviews with seven families following the loss of a child. Several of the participants reported that their body began to feel strange and alien after the loss: 'For some, this unfamiliar sense of their body included a strong sense of being different or as feeling heavy from carrying a heavy load. For others, their body physically hurt. For most, this change lasted only for a short period of time, while for others, their body continued to feel different and changed' (Guðmundsdóttir 2009: 259). Guðmundsdóttir's study is a very welcome empirical contribution, but it does not offer much in the way of theoretical reflection on emotions or the role of the body in grief. The fact that it restricts itself to presenting the participants' oral accounts means that bodily reactions are conceived as something like *symptoms* of intense grief.

A more theoretical phenomenological analysis of grief appears in a recent article by Fuchs (2018), to whom I referred in the previous chapter. As a phenomenologist, Fuchs seeks the 'core structure to the experience of grief' (2018: 45), which has interpersonal, temporal and bodily aspects. Concerning the latter, Fuchs describes grief as an emotion that comes after the initial shock and numbness following bereavement: 'Often the bereaved person closes his eyes or throws his hands before his face in despair, as if to stop vision. This is accompanied by a general bodily exhaustion, passivity, and lack of drive which severely restrict one's initiative and scope of action. Finally, loss of appetite and sleep disturbances also resemble the symptoms of depression' (2018: 46).

When relating to the body in grief, we must understand that it is much more than simply an isolated organism with certain physiological processes. As previously mentioned, grief involves a rupture in the intercorporeality that is created when people interact with each other over long periods of time. Fuchs speaks of a 'dyadic body memory' (2018: 47) that is created in the shared habitualities of long-term interaction, and it is this that is breached by bereavement. Dyadic memory refers to the part of human memory that is shared between the two parties and embedded in their bodily habits. To live with others is, in a sense, to let them in. They become part of us – and vice versa. We carry them in our physical habits, so that when they die, it feels like a mutilation of the body-self. This is not just a short-lived emotional episode, but may fundamentally affect human moods by establishing a lingering undercurrent of loss and lack of the other. Guðmundsdóttir, too, echoes this: 'Following the loss, the body continues to respond to the affordances of the world even if those affordances have ceased to exist' (2009: 265). 'Affordances' refers to the fact that objects and people in the world around us invite us to relate to them in a certain way. These things take the form of encouragements. For phenomenologists, this is not an internal, subjective and mental phenomenon, but something that exists in the actual relationship between the self and the other(s).

In a similar vein, and as discussed in the previous chapter, Ratcliffe argues that a core element of the phenomenology of grief is the loss of 'systems of possibility' (2017: 4). Bereavement robs us of the whole interpersonal

97

system of relating to the other, which otherwise operated as a backdrop to life and meaning. This underpins Attig's central point that grieving is a process of 'relearning the world', in the sense of constructing a new system of possibilities and bodily habits. Both Heidegger and Attig define the self as 'a web of caring connections' (Attig 2004: 348), and phenomenological analyses show that this web is deeply embodied as a system of possibilities for action and meaning. What is still not entirely clear is what it is about emotions like grief that means they are experienced in such a physical manner. The phenomenological descriptions of grief have been restricted to one aspect of the body – how it is felt and experienced. The phenomenological studies mentioned in the previous chapter have been helpful in articulating how grief makes *impressions* on the body as a subject capable of experiences, but are less helpful when it comes to depicting grief's *expression* via the body.

Artistic representations

I now turn to artistic representations (expressions) of the body in grief, which has been a recurring theme in drama, painting, novels and poetry.

In his study of ancient Greek drama, Arnott argues that grief is the most common and best documented emotion in the tragedies (1991: 62). For example, in Euripides' *The Madness of Heracles*, the protagonist murders his wife and children in a moment of madness, and then realises what he has done. He reacts with a grief so intense that he can no longer bear to exist in the world of the living, and conveys this 'by throwing his cloak over his head, removing himself from others' eyes and them from his' (1991: 62). Later, his friend

Greek motif from the sixth century BCE, where the deceased is surrounded by family members and the women ritually tear out their hair

Theseus convinces him to return to the living by uncovering his head. The covering of the head to express grief is a recurring motif in Greek drama. According to Arnott, the Greeks associated life with light – shielding oneself from light is indicative of the death wish that sometimes accompanies intense grief. Perhaps the most famous example of this is Oedipus blinding himself in Sophocles' *Oedipus the King*, 'because he can no longer bear to look upon the world that has betrayed him'. In doing so, he consigns himself to a 'living death' (1991: 63). Less extreme signs of grief in Greek drama include dropping the head and looking at the ground. This is also depicted on decorative Greek vases, 'where the hands are either supporting the lowered head or raised to the forehead in the conventional attitude of melancholy' (1991: 64).

Vincent van Gogh, *At Eternity's Gate* (1890)

As I have already pointed out, this particular use of physiognomy to convey grief recurs throughout the history of art, including in some of the most famous depictions of grief, such as van Gogh's *At Eternity's*

Edvard Munch, *The Sick Child* (1907)

Gate from 1890 or Munch's *The Sick Child* from 1907. In these paintings, the bereaved are portrayed with drooping heads and hands right in front of the face – a typical expression of the embodiment of grief. In both works, the hands seem to form a closed space around the figures, as if they are trying to shield themselves against their loss. However, unlike boxers, who *actively* shield themselves with their hands, these paintings express a more *passive* sense of exhaustion and despair, rather than a readiness to fight. In their study of the

101

relationship between death, memory and material culture, Hallam and Hockey analysed the British cultural
practices (also encountered in many other countries)
associated with widows' clothing. They were expected
to wear black, don veils and cover their hair (Hallam
and Hockey 2001: 69), again emphasising the covering
of the head and face as expressions of grief.

It is sometimes difficult to distinguish 'pure grief'
from other emotions that may follow bereavement and
loss. This, too, is reflected in many historical artworks.
The Greek practice of tearing out your hair and scratch-
ing yourself – and, in more extreme cases, gouging your
eyes out – is clearly a quite aggressive form of despair,
reminiscent of anger. Another close cousin to grief is
sheer physical pain. As described by Nanette Burton
Mongelluzzo: 'The body in grief experiences hardship
in terms of things such as heart rate, respiratory distress, blood pressure, temperature fluctuations (hot and
cold), sensations such as tingling or numbing, aches in
the muscles and/or joints, and at times problems with
gait and balance' (2013: 14). Feelings of depression and
anxiety are also sometimes close to grief. When discussing anxiety, reference is often made to C.S. Lewis's *A
Grief Observed*, which begins with the words: 'No one
ever told me that grief felt so like fear. I am not afraid,
but the sensation is like being afraid. The same fluttering
in the stomach, the same restlessness, the yawning. Keep
on swallowing' (1961: 5). The bodily expression of grief
also closely resembles shame. People tend to feel shame
when they are exposed in front of others, and symbolically try to hide their faces behind their hands (see
Masaccio's fresco depicting Adam and Eve, discussed in
Chapter 2). This is a good example of how our bodies

undergo and express two very different emotions – grief and shame – that can often be distinguished from each other by understanding the social situation in which the body finds itself, instead of just looking at the body in isolation. When a loved one dies, the body turns in on itself, it becomes small and heavy; when someone is ashamed, the body turns away from others.

How can we identify grief and distinguish it from related embodied emotions? My contention is that we need to understand the situation in which the body finds and expresses itself. If we are to distinguish grief from anger, shame, anxiety or physical pain, it is not enough to look at the body in itself, in abstraction from its lifeworld. We must recognise how the body (cognitively) recognises the situation with which it is confronted – and conversely, how the body (communicatively) expresses the situation through posture and movement. This dynamic interplay between the body and the situation – specifically, between impression and expression, cognition and communication – is the key theme of this chapter. In short, we can say that grief is not just embodied, but also embedded, socially and situationally. It may even be capable of being extended across several actors, via socio-material arrangements, as we discuss in the next chapter (see also Brinkmann and Kofod 2018).

Crying

Before moving on to discuss the relationship between emotions and the body more generally – and grief as both embodied and socially embedded – it is worth noting another phenomenon often found in and associated with the grieving body: crying. It is almost superfluous to stress that there is not necessarily any intrinsic connection between crying and grief – we can grieve without crying, and cry without grieving. However, grief is certainly one emotion when, in most cases, crying is both accepted and even normatively preferred. Katz (1999) developed a sophisticated social psychology theory of emotions in general, with a particular focus on crying. The approach supplements phenomenology's focus on experience, the key point of which is that emotional expressions are shaped in anticipation of how they will be perceived (Katz 1999: 5). As such, grief is not simply experienced 'internally', but is co-constituted by socio-cultural 'feeling rules' of which the mourner is self-reflexively aware in their emotional expression.

Katz observes that 'crying is the newborn's way of using voice responsively in social interaction' (1999: 175). Unlike higher mental functions, such as thinking and deliberating – which, according to the school of developmental psychology that goes back to Vygotsky (1978), are the result of more primitive reflexive behaviours – crying in infancy is an intentionally noisy communication. Only later in life, 'despite or perhaps ironically because one has arrived at a mature stage of control over conventional practical problems, one's eyes can begin to well up in unexpected moments of powerlessness as they never did in youth' (Katz 1999: 2). Seen in this light, crying becomes less and less conscious as we grow up. Our tears can also be both of sadness and of joy. We cry not only when in pain, physically or emotionally, but also when elated: 'One is about nonbeing: absence, lack, loss; the other is about an excess of being: being overwhelmed with thankfulness, being overcome with pleasure, being overawed with beauty' (Katz 1999:

182). The latter in particular is usually associated with adulthood (children rarely cry in response to beauty or as an expression of gratitude, although it does happen). Tears of sadness, on the other hand, are related to a kind of existential isolation, which may reiterate themes from early life: 'people may be provoked to sad crying when experiencing not so much a threat to life as evidence of *existential isolation* on the model of an infant's protest against separation from mother' (Katz 1999: 185).

Katz observes that crying is common when people hit the limits of the expressive potential of language (1999: 193). In such cases, crying may be the only means of communication left. The crying body he describes closely resembles the embodiment of grief referred to earlier: 'When people cry, they often scrunch down their faces, press hard to their eyes with a bare hand or cloth, or, doubling over into a balled-up figure, they throw their gaze to the ground. [. . .] Like the instant effects of shutting one's eyes, each of these actions will promote a tacit turn of consciousness toward the bodily inner lining of behaviour' (1999: 213–14). Below, we will see how this aspect of sad crying (shutting our eyes and turning away from the world) was a key element in Sartre's phenomenological theory of emotion, which he associated with a kind of 'magical thinking' (in his words). Summing up Katz's contribution, it might be said that he interprets sad, mournful crying as 'a kind of self-pitying self-regard, a way that one comforts oneself as if from the standpoint of another' (1999: 182). To cry is, in a sense, to experience a temporary loss of the self – a form of emotional externalisation – in order to experience the relief of its return. Crying is a way of comforting ourselves (at least in adults – young children tend to direct it at caregivers). When adults cry, they typically 'close down on themselves, enacting an embrace of themselves as they seek to hold back distress and muffle audible dimensions of their cries' (1999: 187). The phenomenologists referred to above describe how grief is felt in the body, and how the body then expresses that emotion to others. Social-psychological studies of the communicative effects of crying complement these descriptions by analysing how physical expressions (such as crying) can return to and comfort the individual and have a consoling effect on them.

Back to the question: What are emotions?

At this juncture, we must depart briefly from our discussion of grief and the body, and ask a more general question: what are emotions? Which theory of emotions is needed to explain how they are 'carried out' in the specific situation? There is much to learn from the phenomenological descriptions of grief by Fuchs and others, because they emphasise how grief is registered in the body. There is also much to learn from social-psychological analyses such as those by Katz, which focus on the crying, grieving body as (self-)communicating. Our first-hand emotional experience tells us that humans are both the subject and object of our life processes. As Katz puts it, emotions are 'not just done to but also done by a person' (1999: 1). Can this also be understood in phenomenological terms?

A classic text on this theme is Sartre's philosophical theory of emotions (Sartre 2006; the following is based on Brinkmann and Musaeus 2012). Sartre pitted his theory against James's early psychological theory of emotions, according to which 'bodily changes follow directly the perception of the exciting fact, and that our feeling of the same changes as they occur is the emotion' (James 1983: 1065). According to James, therefore, we are wrong to assume that we cry because we are sorry to have lost our fortune, or that we run away from the dangerous bear because we are frightened. According to his hypothesis, 'this order of sequence is incorrect' (1983: 1065). It is more correct to say that 'we feel sorry because we cry, angry because we strike, afraid because we tremble, and not that we cry, strike, or tremble, because we are sorry, angry, or fearful' (1983: 1066). Although there are few today who wholeheartedly support James' theory, it has nonetheless affected some of the most influential contemporary thinkers. Damasio (1999), for example, explicitly acknowledges his debt to James and shares the view that emotions are largely a reflection of changes to our bodily state.

Sartre's phenomenological study describes emotions as centrally directed at objects, rather than (as James and Damasio have argued) at changed bodily states. Sartre goes along with Heidegger's existential phenomenology, according to which human beings should first and foremost be thought of as creatures who *understand*. Sartre says that an emotion 'is not an accident, it is a mode of our conscious existence, one of the ways in which consciousness understands (in Heidegger's sense of *Verstehen*) its Being-in-the-World' (2006: 61). Emotions are therefore cognitive; in Sartre's words, they are 'accompanied by belief' (2006: 49). If we feel fear, we believe – or fear (which here are synonymous) – that something dreadful will happen. This belief or conviction is inseparable from the emotion and vice versa. While emotions cannot be equated with purely cognitive beliefs (such as two plus two equals four), they do embrace beliefs and assessments of objects. According to the cognitive view, the belief may be true (if the danger is real) or it may be false and even pathological (if there is nothing to fear). In short, emotions are ways of 'apprehending the world' (Sartre 2006: 35). They are significant because they refer to something and involve understanding (2006: 12). Sartre's term for this emotional form of apprehending the world is *magic*, which emphasises the fact that emotions do not signify physical properties of the world, but instead alert us to the meanings of situations in our lifeworld. Sartre explains, for example, that the meaning of fear 'is to negate something in the external world by means of magical behaviour, and will go so far as to annihilate itself in order to annihilate the object also' (2006: 43). Passive fear, therefore, consists of seeing a dangerous object (e.g. a wild animal), in response to which our legs give way, we turn pale and possibly even faint, which is a way of avoiding (or annihilating, to use Sartre's dramatic terminology) the object (by obliterating our own consciousness). That we relate to objects 'magically' in our emotional lives means that objects do not just mechanically trigger bodily reactions (which we then experience and label as emotions), but rather that they are functions relative to the social reality in which we participate as embodied, emotional agents.

Sartre's idea of emotions as involving 'magical thinking' is not readily applicable to the whole repertoire of human emotions, but it seems particularly relevant to grief. Appositely, Joan Didion's – rightfully – celebrated grief memoir (written after she had lost her husband) is titled *The Year of Magical Thinking*. She describes precisely how her grief made her understand the world in a new, 'magical' way: 'I needed to be alone so that he could come back. This was the beginning of my year of magical thinking' (2005: 33). For Didion, magical thinking is both a belief that the dead will return – 'I could not give away the rest of his shoes. I stood there for a moment, then realised why: he would need shoes if he was to return' (2005: 37) – and also about the loss of a system of possibilities (as mentioned earlier), which plays all sorts of tricks on the bereaved individual who is used to the physical presence of the other after years of living together. This magical thinking is also expressed in a tangible manner by the body, in the way that the hands cover the face as if to say, 'It is not real! If I turn away from it, look down, cover my eyes, the loss will not be real. I cannot bear to look at it!'

Sartre's phenomenology clearly demonstrates that emotions are not mental objects 'within us', causally produced by bodily changes. On the contrary, they are ways in which people understand situations and events normatively (understand what they should do). Helm summarises this view of emotions, and concludes that they are 'essentially feelings of things as good or bad in a certain way' (2009: 249). However, goodness and bad- ness here should be thought of as properties not of our subjectivities (which would lead to a Jamesian account in which emotions consist of subjectively registered bodily changes), but of the objects to which our emotions are directed. When a person feels fear, they feel bad because something pains them, but that 'something' does not need to be (and rarely is) part of the body. Rather, it is (to borrow Helm's example) the danger that frost presents to the person's garden (2009: 249). Cockburn, in line with other philosophers in the Wittgensteinian tradition, reaches the following conclusion: 'To feel a particular emotion may be to recognise the character of a situation with which one is confronted' (2009: 133). In this sense, emotions are sources of knowledge about the values and significances of objects and events in the world (Lesch 2001). Like all other forms of knowledge, they may be more or less misguided, which indicates a certain fundamental normativity. As we have seen several times, grief reveals our love for a person who has died, and therefore it represents a recognition of the loss. Grief is not a passive, mechanical reaction, but a responsive understanding of a relationship that has ended (or at least changed). This responsive understanding is, as we have seen, felt (cognised) in the body and expressed (communicated) by the body.

The cognitive approach to emotions that emerged from Aristotle has been revitalised in recent years, especially by Nussbaum in philosophy and by the appraisal theorists in psychology (Moors et al. 2013). Appraisal theories are convincing in terms of the cognitive aspect of emotions, but much less convincing when it comes to the role of the body in emotional processes. I therefore conclude this chapter by trying to develop a theoretical perspective on the body that makes it relevant to the appraisal theories. The point is to arrive at an understanding of the body's role in the impression-expression dynamic. This is, I think, applicable to grief as an emotion – we understand grief to be bodily, as it makes an *impression* on the body (almost literally, as we appear to become smaller, heavier), but at the same time there is an *expression* of grief through the body, which in turn leaves an impression on others. However, this presupposes a viable idea of the body and of its role in emotional and cognitive processes. So what is a body? As we will see in the next section, the body is several different things at once.

What is a body?

Arguably, the most influential account of the body in philosophy and psychology stems from Merleau-Ponty (2012). In his philosophical writings, he sought to develop a more adequate phenomenology capable of overcoming the objectification of the body in modern science. Much of the success of modern medicine can be attributed to its perspective on the body as a piece of living machinery. This is, of course, not entirely wrong. The mechanical perspective is perfectly legitimate when it comes to, for example, fixing a broken bone. But the body is more than just a biological organism. Merleau-Ponty showed that it is, above all, a 'lived body'. In other words, we act in and have experiences of the world through our body. When I move my arm to pick something up, the experience is not one of first making the decision with the mind and then moving the body's arm as two separate processes. No, I move my arm when I want to – the will to do so resides, in a sense, within my arm. My arm, as a part of my body, is also a part of me as a subject – it is in a way 'mental', and not just physical. The phenomenological experience of 'the lived body' refers to the phenomenological experience of *being* the body.

As far as death and bereavement in general goes, the phenomenological perspective on the body was taken up by Clive Seale, who combines it with a focus on socially constructed cultural processes. According to his sociological account, all social and cultural life is, ultimately, 'a human construction in the face of death', which is brought about by a 'realisation of embodiment' (1998: 8). Seale argues that human social life must be understood in the context of embodiment, which is essentially a recognition of the finitude of the body. In order to understand the role of the body more specifically in relation to grief after bereavement, we can refer to the work of key phenomenological embodiment researchers. Building on Merleau-Ponty, Mark Johnson argues that we need at least five different ways of looking at the body in order to arrive at a full understanding of it – and of its emotions (2007: 275–7; see also Brinkmann 2017a, in which these approaches are discussed in greater depth). The following perspectives on the body illustrate the different dimensions of embodied grief (of which the phenomenological perspective ought to be accorded a certain degree of precedence):

(1) The body as a biological organism: This is the body as it is studied by physiology and anatomy and healed by medical science. It is the body as an organism, consisting of blood vessels and nerves, hormones and organs. There is no doubt that most instances of grief involve changes in the physiological systems of the organism. However, as pointed out by Merleau-Ponty, when we view the body based on traditional natural science methodology, we turn it into an object that does not fit into our system of experience (Merleau-Ponty 2012: 63). Viewed solely as a biological organism, the

body is a collection of tissues and organs. This perspective is useful for a variety of reasons – when we have to perform surgery on it, for example – but it is inadequate when it comes to the role the body plays in understanding existential situations like bereavement, and how we use it to express our grief, because the biological body does not understand or express *meaning* (e.g. the meaning of loss, death and love).

(2) The ecological body: The body as connected with its environment. Although we tend to assume that it is easy to differentiate the body from its environment – the skin acts as a boundary – this is actually a somewhat arbitrary and problematic idea (Mol 2008). For example, the body depends on nourishment and oxygen, which are constantly moving into and out of it, and a large part of the body is made up of micro-organisms, which are independent beings that 'live' inside of us. Tools and technology can also be said to be part of the body. Such technologies are not just limited to obvious ones such as prosthetic limbs, but also, for example, a visually impaired person's cane or glasses. These can, with a certain degree of justification, be said to belong to the body and its psychological functions – at least when it is viewed as an ecological body closely related to its surroundings (Brinkmann and Kofod 2018). Johnson concludes that the body is not separate from its surroundings, and that any boundary we draw between the two reflects an attempt to bolster a specific viewpoint (2007: 276). When the body is viewed ecologically, we must consider it and the environment as two aspects of a single, continuous process. As I have argued above, in grief, the embodied self understands the situation in which it finds itself as a result of the loss of both the

other person and of the 'system of possibilities' associated with them. Conversely, the body's expressions
function as a context marker for the bereavement situation. Grief as an embodied emotion is not separate
from the situation, rather it is deeply embedded in the
contexts of the lifeworld and the entirety of the material
culture surrounding death and bereavement, to which I
return in the next chapter (see also Hallam and Hockey
2001).

(3) The phenomenological body: This is our body as
we live and experience it, where it forms the basis for
our experience of a meaningful world (Johnson 2007:
276). The phenomenological body is the body as we
know it prior to our knowledge of scientific theories
about it (e.g. theories about the body as a biological
organism). In other words, it is the body as it is experienced pre-reflexively and pre-theoretically. This
dimension of experience is exactly what phenomenological studies address. Above, I provided some recent
examples of studies from this perspective, by Fuchs and
others, that look at the body during grief and how it
involves elements of heaviness, passivity, constriction
and withdrawal.

(4) The social body: The body exists not just in physical or biological worlds, but also in a social world. The
body and its dispositions are shaped by our social interactions with others, from the moment we are born until
the day we die. We are social, intersubjective beings
right from the outset. Recent psychological research
on infants and their interactions with caregivers has
revealed some of the ways in which the body and its
habits are formed through early, complex patterns of
interaction (a classic source is Trevarthen 1993). From

this perspective, the grieving body is one that has experienced a rupture from a significant social bond, and is therefore cut off from intersubjective relations with a loved one. Bereavement disrupts intercorporeality and demands the formation of new bodily habits. As such, 'grief work' is not just about crafting meaningful new life narratives, but also about adjusting the way we comport ourselves physically in a changed social world. It should also be noted that grief is not simply experienced as the rupturing of a significant social bond that exists in isolation from other intersubjective relations. Rather, we share this experience with others – our families, friends and colleagues. This aspect is rarely addressed in studies of grief, although there is widespread awareness of the role of social groups in providing emotional support.

(5) The cultural body: This is closely related to the social perspective, but focuses more on cultural differences regarding appropriate and inappropriate bodily behaviours, including in connection with grief. The body is always and unavoidably enmeshed in a network of standards that govern appearance, size, clothing, decoration and movement. For example, there are cultural differences not only in terms of masculine and feminine ways of moving, but also in terms of phenomena that appear to be purely physical, such as a flavour to which we respond positively. Culture is not something that affects the body from the outside, rather the body is cultural per se by virtue of the way it appears, poses and gestures. In this chapter, I have tried to account for some of the long history of bodily comportment in grief stretching back (at least) to the ancient Greeks, but we should also acknowledge the intercultural

differences relating to the impression and expression of grief. For example, Scheper-Hughes's (1993) ethnographic and social-anthropological study of a Brazilian shanty town shows that specific socio-cultural factors (i.e. an extremely high child mortality rate) lead to a degree of indifference when young children die. In this context, grief is impressed on bodies in a way that is quite different from places in the world that are safer and more affluent. Examples of differences in the bodily expression of grief are perhaps most visible in the huge variation that exists in funeral practices between different epochs, cultures and religions. However, there does seem to be a core repertoire of bodily grief expressions, as argued in a recent account of death and bereavement across cultures: 'Crying, fear and anger are so common as to be virtually ubiquitous and most cultures provide social sanction for the expression of these emotions in the funeral rites and customs of mourning which follow bereavement' (Parkes, Laungani and Young 2015: 5). The fact that expressions of grief are almost universal also explains why we are able to re-enact ancient Greek tragedies today, a couple of millennia after they were first performed, and still understand the grief felt by the characters.

Digression on the Danish play SAVN

To illustrate the physical immediacy of the experience of grief, I now briefly digress from the phenomenological theory to discuss a theatre performance about the experience of loss. In November 2017, I and the research group from the 'Culture of Grief' project attended

an avant-garde theatrical performance about grief
by a group called CoreAct (the following is based on
Brinkmann et al., not yet published). The group create
their art through systematic research (in this case, via
interviews with the bereaved, as well as reflexive self-
study of their own grief). As researchers, we decided to
study both the development of the play and its performance, and to report our experiences as members of the
audience. While CoreAct makes research-based theatre
art, we as a research group wanted to try our hands at
art-based research.

We first became aware of the performance about
grief when I was contacted in November 2016 by Anika
Barkan and Helene Kvint, who make up CoreAct. At
that time, reports had started to appear in the media
that our research project would start studying grief
from a phenomenological and cultural-psychological
perspective in 2017. Barkan and Kvint had been studying grief for a long time, and had collected numerous
accounts from bereaved people. These and their own
experiences with loss formed the basis of their play,
SAVN (which translates as longing, privation, missing
or need), subtitled *A Tribute to Grief*. As a group of
qualitative researchers, we had not originally intended
to team up with artists, but it seemed appropriate in
this case because the artistic study of the phenomenon
seemed to complement our own, more conventional
and linear approach really well. I held several meet-
ings with Barkan and Kvint, and a year after the initial
contact, the whole research team went to Copenhagen
to meet the CoreAct team and attend a performance.
Afterwards, we would also interview the other three
actors as well as members of the audience. One outcome

of this was a new research method that we call multi-perspectival ethnography.

It turned out that the various different research perspectives neatly reflected the four different strands that ran through the performance. The performance was site-specific, in a building in Copenhagen called *Slottet* (the Castle). It took place on the top floor, in many different rooms connected by a long corridor. We entered the building under a large neon sign saying SAVN in purple capital letters. The sign acted as a context marker, which invited the participants to interpret each tableau in the performance in the light of their own experience(s) of loss and longing. When entering the building, we were each asked to don one of four

Scene from *SAVN*. Reproduced with permission from Teater Grob's official website:
https://www.grob.dk/forestilling/savn

name badges – Kim, Nor, Mai or Sonni – representing four ways of moving through the performance. There were forty-five people in the audience, divided into four groups (of varying sizes). We ten researchers were divided up like everybody else. This division of the audience meant that not everyone saw all of the scenes, and not everyone watched them in the same order. As Barkan and Kvint explained, the artists had deliberately sought to create fragments – intense tableaux in which human beings expressed grief in various ways with their bodies and voices, accompanied by sounds and music (one actor, dressed like a raven, was a musician who played different instruments), but without any over-arching storyline. *SAVN* is a performance without narrative, without plot. It is a deliberate attempt to convey the sense of loss, despair and existential fragmentation associated with grief.

CoreAct's aim was to establish grief's presence in the various rooms, but without the usual temporal contexts presented in novels, films and grief memoirs, and without the classic three-act narrative structure, or even the sequential stages of grief as described in self-help literature. The four groups spent almost two hours moving through the rooms, witnessing and participating in these grief tableaux. Afterwards, everyone gathered in a single room with the cast. The actors then initiated a (rehearsed) discussion about how they would like to be buried. They referred to all sorts of different burial rituals and ceremonies from all over the world, which helped to lighten the mood in quite an uplifting way, sparking laughter among both the audience and the actors themselves:

119

Anika: What about you Helene, what are you going to do?

Helene: I will have my bowels sucked out of me, with two straws through the nose, so there are no worms that can eat me. I'll be like the mummies in ancient Egypt.

Anika: Yes, it's good, but I'd rather be mummified in my favourite clothes, like in Sicily, and then suspended from hooks, close to others, so I won't be alone in death. Anders, did you know that about every tenth person in Denmark dies totally alone?

Lukas: When you mentioned Sicily, I remembered Madagascar. Every five years I'd like to be dug up, so people can dance with my body throughout the village.

Anders: If I can't get on a totem pole, I'll be cremated like a Hindu – on a fire by the river.

Helene: Yes, yes, I would also like to be cremated like an ancient Hindu, and then my widow will throw herself into the flames.

This ending – with everyone together – created a sense of solidarity that had been totally absent from the previous tableaux, in which the actors were largely alienated from each other (and from the audience). Everyone was alone with their grief, and the actors rarely spoke directly to each other. Now, we were all included, together with the actors, creating a sense of togetherness and humour – perhaps the only real weapons we have against the absurd reality of death. As the poet Naja Marie Aidt describes it, in simple, almost programmatic terms, in her book about the loss of her son, *When Death Takes Something From You Give It Back*: 'Community is the only option' (2017: 144). One actor requested some New Orleans jazz, a phone rang and we left the room. Out in the hallway, we heard the recording of an old woman's creaky voice:

The Body in Grief – Grief in the Body

When I say or think of your name, you exist
Everything ends when those who love you die
As long as they live, you are loved
As long as you are loved, you exist.

This was followed by applause. The actors then served everyone coffee and cake, and hung around to discuss the play and its themes with the audience. I do not think a single person went straight home – everyone stayed for a while to talk. Several people were visibly moved, which according to the actors was quite a common occurrence.

After the play, all of the researchers who attended wrote down their immediate, fragmented impressions of a performance that seemed designed to create a sense of chaos and confusion. I wrote:

It all feels chaotic. We are led from one room to the next by a man dressed like a raven. I try to connect the different scenes: who has died? Is it the mother? Is she a ghost now? But my attempts at making sense of it break down again right away. There is no story. Or, if there is, it is a story of no story. I become frustrated, perhaps even a little bit angry. I feel a little disappointed. But in one room, my feelings change. I see Anders, the oldest of the male actors, sitting on a sofa. The sofa is well worn. Many people have probably used it to sit and talk, take naps, watch TV, and perhaps to make love. Anders then turns to the large button on the sofa pillow and touches it. He begins to caress it, and then he embraces the whole pillow, and finally the entire sofa. His movements are slow and gentle. It is an erotic scene, but Anders is fully dressed, and he is all alone on the sofa. He performs a quiet ballet on the sofa, with little drama, sometimes with his eyes closed. He is probably imagining the person he loves – and has made love to on

121

the sofa. But now that person is no longer there, and her or his absence is striking. Anders shows us love without a loved one. His body and its movements are attuned to someone who is gone. It is a scene of soundless despair, and it is really beautiful. My fleeting feelings of anger and disappointment vanish. I am left with a bittersweet feeling of grief. I experience a strong urge to get my phone out and call my wife.

In his silent performance, which involves only the body, Anders shows what longing and need – in this case, erotic and romantic love – can look like in grief. The idea that the beloved deceased lives on in the survivor's physicality is found in countless descriptions of grief. For example, Naja Marie Aidt writes about her late son:

> It's a physical feeling.
> He is inside me.
> He is inside my body.
> I bear his spirit in my body.
> I bear him again inside my body.
> As when he was in my womb.
> But now I bear *his entire life*.
> I bear your entire life. (2017: 154)

Although *SAVN* and Aidt's book convey the experience of grief in very different ways, what they have in common is that they waive the need for narrative and connecting plot, instead showing – presenting – the experience of grief more directly. If grief is about absence, confusion, breakdown, fragmentation and loss of meaning, then this disjointed display is almost an objective representation of the emotion. There is an almost perfect correspondence between phenomenon and representation, which means that art has the potential to present emotions like grief in at least as objective a manner as scientific perspectives. As the qualitative researcher Ron Pelias put it, 'Science is the act of looking at a tree and seeing lumber. Poetry is the act of looking at a tree and seeing a tree' (2004: 9).

Hans Ulrich Gumbrecht conducts research into literature and culture. Drawing inspiration from phenomenologists such as Heidegger, he developed the concept of *presence* to describe how art can help us to understand phenomena (Gumbrecht 2004). He argues that art plays a role in understanding via its ability to connect to the body by means of a spatial presence, mediated by writing, music, visual arts or drama. Gumbrecht juxtaposes presence and meaning, and accuses human science of focusing almost exclusively on seeking to interpret the meaning of cultural phenomena. Meaning is obviously not unimportant, but by focusing on it we overlook the 'layers' of culture that are all about sensuality, the body and physical presence. If we hear a piece of beautiful music, any goose bumps that arise will probably not have been caused by interpreting its meaning. Or if we hear a poem being recited, a different understanding of it will be communicated through rhyme, rhythm and intonation than if we read the words silently.

There is a material dimension to our bodily being-in-the-world that creates what Gumbrecht calls *presence-effects*. Presence is produced whenever 'the impact that "present" objects have on human bodies is being initiated or intensified' (2004: xiii). It consists of a non-interpretive understanding of the world, in which we stand in an immediate, physical relationship to situations and objects. To achieve this, we must, in Gumbrecht's words, 'try to pause for a moment before we begin to make sense' (2004: 126). However, as beings who seek meaning, we find this difficult to do. This is where art plays an important role – not just in generating meaning, but also in presenting phenomena that do not immediately appear to be meaningful. Grief is just such a phenomenon. It is, of course, meaningful in the sense that it is about homeless love (and what is more meaningful than love?), but it also occurs precisely when we experience loss, which itself is meaningless. Those fond of paradoxes might describe grief as meaningful meaninglessness – as is made clear in various aesthetic representations. The word aesthetics comes from the Greek *aisthetike*, which means sensing. Despite the fact that in this book I argue that emotions cannot be reduced to mere sensations, there is no doubt that we need to understand the physical, sensory dimension that is *also* present in psychological phenomena like grief.

Conclusions: The appraising body in grief

In this chapter I have addressed the body in grief. I have argued that grief is at once an emotion that is impressed on and felt through the body, and something we express using our bodies in social situations. The body is at once physiological, ecological, phenomenological, social and cultural. Like other emotions, grief involves an appraisal of the situation in which you find yourself (in this case, loss). As such, it has a cognitive component, but it also has social and communicative components, as bodies express grief through specific postures, gestures, gazes and ways of comporting themselves. These have been depicted in the arts since the Greek tragedies, in famous paintings and in modern drama. While some emotion theorists have emphasised isolated facial expressions (e.g. Ekman 1992), in this chapter we have seen that grief involves the whole body, and is archetypically depicted by a hanging head and hands closed in front of the face. Likewise, crying is a significant bodily manifestation of grief that serves a self-comforting function as part of a dynamic interplay between expression and impression.

Phenomenological studies provide an understanding of the experiential side of grief as something carried in the body. In particular, Sartre's phenomenology of emotion emphasised the object-directedness of emotional life. For the same reason, we do not feel emotions by noting our bodily reactions – as James and Damasio would have it – rather, we use our bodies to read and understand the situations in which we find ourselves. Contrary to the Jamesian perspective, the body and the brain do not form a 'theatre' in which emotions appear and are observed by the mind (an idea also criticised by Wetherell 2012). Instead, we use the entirety of our embodied subjectivity to understand the world in which we live and our relationships with others. When our loved ones are irrevocably gone, we understand this through our bodies. We have lost the system of possibilities in which we interacted with the other, which was impressed on us in the form of embodied habits. The appraisal theorists share the same cognitive view of emotions put forward by Sartre, who sees emotions as intentional and capable of revealing the meanings of situations and objects. However, they lack an adequate explanation of the role of the body, which I have tried to provide here.

I concluded the chapter by borrowing from Johnson's recent Merleau-Pontian perspectives on the body. All of these are relevant to the various manifestations of grief, but the phenomenological 'lived body' is particularly significant. I suggest that, in order to understand how an emotion like grief can be both cognitive and embodied, what is required is an integration of cognitive appraisal theories of emotions and phenomenological theories of the body. The process of cognitive appraisal is not carried out by a disembodied mind, but by an embodied, embedded person who exists in the world as part of a network of caring relations. Grief is the bodily impression/expression of the understanding of how these relations can be severed. For that reason, the capacity to feel grief is foundational for human subjectivity and intersubjectivity, as I addressed more fully in the chapter on grief as a foundational emotion. Understanding the role of the body in grief can also be very important in the context of the professional help that is becoming increasingly common after bereavement. Such help should – when it is justified – not only address the symbolic and narrative mental processes, but also the more habitual and embodied aspects of our existence, issues which I hope research will take up in future.

5

The Ecology of Grief

You are at a funeral, having just lost someone that you really love, perhaps a parent.[12] The coffin is in the middle of the room. Every time you look at it, you think of the person inside and how much you miss them.[13] You listen to the minister talk about them, and your eyes fill with tears. When the organ plays a beautiful psalm, everybody sings along. You try to join in, but it makes you cry. In the days prior to the funeral, the family discussed what it would be like. You shared memories of the deceased, looked at old photos, and maybe even shared out important heirlooms. Maybe the lost loved one was an avid bass player, and the sight of their favourite instrument fills you with a strange blend of sadness and gratitude. In the days, weeks and years to come, you keep returning to this and other objects, you keep telling stories about the person – perhaps to your children and grandchildren – and you keep looking at photos. You might take an interest in books written by other bereaved people, and find a certain comfort in the fact that almost everyone experiences something similar. If the grief keeps weighing you down to the extent it is impossible to return to an active life, you might join a bereavement support group – or your doctor may even diagnose you with 'complicated grief'.

Most of the contents of this little introductory vignette are fairly uncontroversial, even insignificant at first glance. They are bits and pieces of experiences that are commonplace when a person dies and others are left to mourn their passing. In this chapter, however, we will take what is common and uncontroversial and interpret it in the light of a topical theory about the human mind and emotions. This approach may seem somewhat strange at first, because what I argue is that the process of grieving described above is best understood not as a psychological process 'inside the mind', but rather as an *extended* psychological process that involves objects and persons in our environment as constituent parts of the emotion. As I showed in the last chapter, grief manifests itself in an environment that is both social and material – a kind of ecology of grief.[14]

Even though the hypothesis of 'the extended mind' is becoming increasingly well established in psychology and other human sciences, few scholars have yet applied it to human emotional life (notable exceptions include Krueger 2014; Slaby 2014; Colombetti and Krueger 2015; Griffiths and Scarantino 2009), and no one has so far (to my knowledge) discussed it in relation to grief specifically. The extended mind hypothesis states that objects in the environment (notebooks or calendars, for instance) function as a part of the mind, and are closely involved in cognitive processes. Much in the same way as a tennis racket is a necessary object in the process of playing tennis, various other artefacts and technologies are necessary components in human cognitive processes.

When we find our way using GPS, take notes or arrange the inventory in our workplace, we are using and developing an ecology that helps us generate knowledge and solve problems. The mind is therefore not just situated in the head, it is embodied in organisms, embedded in contexts and environmentally extended and distributed.

Let me begin by introducing the extended mind hypothesis and the idea of extended emotions before applying them specifically to an analysis of grief as an extended emotion, and seeking to explain the hypothesis via the ecological concept of an *affective niche* within which grief is usually 'scaffolded' and enacted (I will explain these terms in more detail). The affective niche is a concept that links the person to their environment and makes emotional states possible. In the case of grief, this might involve individual material 'scaffoldings', such as gravestones, clothing, belongings and pictures of the deceased, as well as collective ones, such as social rituals and ceremonies, communal singing and other grief practices, some of which were illustrated in the opening vignette. I would argue that more attention should be paid to the materially extended and socially distributed aspects of grief. This is difficult in cultural contexts such as Denmark and the West in general, which have a much more individualistic approach to emotion, but we must understand that an emotion like grief is supported by and takes place in an ecology. The system of affective niches is, in reality, a whole grief ecology.

Grief

The extended mind hypothesis

In general, the extended mind hypothesis can be traced back 200 years to philosophers such as G.W.F. Hegel, for whom the individual's mind is dependent upon the operations of social practices and institutions (Crisafi and Gallagher 2010). The 'subjective spirit' is in fact related to the objective, as represented by social institutions. In more recent times, the philosopher Hilary Putnam developed the theory of 'externalism' in the 1970s. For Putnam, meaning and significance do not reside in the head, but are a matter of how the outside world is constituted (the following sections are based on Brinkmann 2009). In his famous thought experiment, Putnam (1975) postulated the existence of a twin Earth that is completely identical to our own planet, except that the molecular structure of its water is not H_2O, but XYZ. In both worlds, all of the observable properties of the water are the same – wet, quenches thirst, freezes at 0°, boils at 100° and so on. Putnam then asks: if a person on Earth and their counterpart on twin Earth are completely identical, molecule for molecule, and both think about water, do their thoughts have the same meaning? Are they thinking about the same thing? Putnam says no. The person on Earth is thinking about H_2O, while his counterpart is thinking about XYZ. This is the case even if they do not personally know the molecular structure of water. What they are thinking about does *not* depend on their knowledge or mental representations (the internal), but on the nature of the physical world (the external). It is not a difference in people's 'heads' that determines whether they

130

are thinking about one thing or the other, but a difference in their environment. This thought experiment led to the concept of *externalism*: that the meaning of our thoughts, utterances and attitudes is not determined by something inside the individual, but by something outside of them. In more general terms, the mental 'content' of our psyche can only be grasped by looking at the material things 'around' the psyche.

While the discussion about meaning and Earth/twin Earth is still ongoing, other forms of externalism have also emerged. Putnam's externalism might be dubbed *semantic* externalism, because it relates to meaning, and only indirectly to the mental as a whole. One of the best known advocates of the externalist view today is the philosopher Andy Clark. His externalism is not only semantic, but also *psychological*. Clark (2008) argues that we humans are 'natural born cyborgs' who, through technology, can 'supersize' our minds. We use things and technologies – everything from glasses that help us see better, to scientific instruments, books, charts, etc. – to expand and refine our cognitive processes. Clark's theory might more accurately be called 'active externalism' (Clark and Chalmers 1998). Whereas Putnam's externalism was passive, because neither the individuals themselves nor the environment on either of the planets did anything to differentiate between the two (instead, a static difference in the environment resulted in a difference in the meaning of the thought), *active* externalism focuses on how people and environments are actively and reciprocally involved in cognitive and, more broadly, mental processes. The conclusion is that cognitive processes are not exclusively in the mind, but extend to our use of technology and artefacts.

A host of examples illustrate this conclusion, but we will look first at a typical cognitive task often studied in experimental psychology: mental rotation. This is an exercise in which we imagine the currently hidden sides of three-dimensional figures by rotating them in our 'mind's eye'. Imagine that you are tasked with determining whether a three-dimensional shape on a computer screen is the same as another shape when seen from the other side. To find out, you can either rotate the shape 'mentally' or on the computer screen. Is it fair to say that only the first situation involves a mental component? What if, in the future, we have the ability to artificially enhance our brains with neural implants that will enable us to perform mental rotation as if on a computer screen, only 'internally'? There are no good arguments as to why there is any difference in principle between the three scenarios, regardless of whether we rotate the figure 'purely mentally', using the computer screen or using a neural implant. The technological solutions that make it easier (for most people) to imagine three-dimensional shapes from the other side are, in this situation, just as much a part of our mind as the brain structures that usually facilitate mental rotation.

The same applies to something as simple as a notebook. If a patient with incipient Alzheimer's copes with day-to-day life by jotting down relevant pieces of information, then the notebook is a substitute for the 'brainpower' that the same person used to use to remember things – but there is no reason to believe that the notebook is any less mentally relevant just because it is external and exists outside of the person's skull. Imagine that somebody asks the patient whether he knows how high the Eiffel Tower is. He says yes, but has to consult the notebook to provide the correct answer – '300 metres'. We have no reason to claim that the person concerned did not know the height of the famous tower. The notebook plays the same mental role for that person as memory does for someone whose brain functions in such a way that they are able to use *it* (the brain) to remember the height of the Eiffel Tower. Someone who is not suffering from Alzheimer's may at first struggle to remember the answer, and might say 'Wait . . . I need to think . . . I've got it: 300 metres!' It is correct to say that this person knew the answer all the time. So did the patient who had to look it up in their notebook. This is the basic principle of externalism.

A counter-argument sometimes raised against externalism is that an artefact such as a notebook should not be regarded as part of the mind because it is physically separate from the person, and may even be located some distance away. We can lose a notebook, but not our brain, as the saying goes. In a sense, this is patently wrong, precisely because the Alzheimer's patient *can* be said to have 'lost' a bit of their brain. It is also more generally questionable to require that something be physically part of our person in order for it to be called mental. Somebody who needs glasses to read a book is still able to read, even if they left their glasses at the top of the Eiffel Tower. A visually impaired person's cane is still the same technology that allows them to extend their recognition of the world around them, whether the stick is currently in use or they have set it aside. There is no point in making physical proximity to the person's body the criterion of whether a material thing is considered part of the individual's psyche. Instead, what matters is whether the artefact plays a relevant functional role in relation to the person's ability to carry out specific mental tasks. However, this conclusion is not without its problems either. It entails an almost infinite expansion of things that might be said to belong to the mental realm – all kinds of things can play all kinds of functional roles, large or small, in almost any conceivable mental process. For example, the notebook is manufactured from a specific material that is processed by specific people through specific social practices. Should every element of this be thought of as included in the person's mind? Clearly, this sounds absurd. The challenge for the externalist perspective is how to *delimit* the parts of an organism's environment that are relevant to its mental processes.

We could also imagine another future scenario in which everyone is constantly online, perhaps via a neural interface, and can instantly download any kind of factual information from a collective knowledge bank – a bit like how people use Google today. Would we all then effectively know everything – or at least, everything stored in the collective knowledge bank? It is not clear whether we would talk about it in those terms. However, we would probably have to revolutionise our idea of what constitutes a mental process. Many of us already use Google for a variety of tasks – to gather factual information, as a dictionary, to help with various other jobs. Instant online access from anywhere at any time would constitute a huge boost to our cognitive capacity.

In other words, externalism has a boundary problem – where are the limits of the mind, if everything is part of our mental processes? My proposed solution to this problem is to downplay the whole 'localisation' discussion, at least in the strict sense. Indeed, it may be fundamentally problematic to ask *where* the mind is situated (in the head, in the body, elsewhere?). If we instead approach mental phenomena, including emotions, not as 'things' or 'objects', but instead as abilities or capacities to act, think and feel (Bennett and Hacker 2003), then the question is not *where* the mind is located (because abilities and capacities are not situated in physical space), but rather *what kind of mediators* – intermediaries – make it possible for people to act, think and feel in certain ways (Brinkmann 2011). From this perspective, extended minds (in externalist theory) are *mediators* that constitute a person's range of skills and abilities, enabling them to recognise features of the world, solve problems, act and respond emotionally to what is happening.

Extended emotions

If our knowledge is not just 'in our head', but is also distributed among the various artefacts in our environment, is the same also true of our feelings? When we discuss whether it makes sense to say that emotions such as grief can be 'extended', it is crucial to do so based on a specific definition of emotion, since the concept can be interpreted in many different ways. Based on certain definitions, it makes little sense to say that emotions can be extended. Under other definitions, however, the extendedness of emotions is absolutely central. This section looks at the latter type of definition, as discussed in the previous chapter.

Robert Zajonc's (1984) well-known theory emphasises

the immediate affective response of an organism and downplays the role of cognitive and evaluative procedures in emotional life. According to Zajonc, emotions are, in a sense, the organism's 'inner'. They are by definition not extended, as they can be fully understood by looking at what is going on under the skin of the person. Similarly, Antonio Damasio's influential neo-Jamesian theory sees emotions as something 'internal' in the organism. As previously mentioned, he sees emotion as 'a specifically caused transient change of the organism state' (Damasio 1999: 282). He says: 'Feeling an emotion is a simple matter. It consists of having mental images arising from the neural patterns which represent the changes in body and brain that make up an emotion' (1999: 280). We see here the clear legacy of William James, who in *The Principles of Psychology* reasoned that feelings are records of bodily changes. In other words, according to James, we are sad because we cry, rather than vice versa. Although the theories of Zajonc, Damasio and James differ to some extent, they are united in their internalism, i.e. the idea that what we refer to as emotions in psychology are processes that can be understood by looking exclusively at what takes place in the individual organism.

By now, it should be apparent that this book adopts a quite different view of emotions (I criticised Damasio's theory in Brinkmann 2006a). What is missing from the internalist theories is, first and foremost, and as previously analysed in this book, recognition of the intentional, evaluative and object-oriented nature of emotions. One almost trivial (but nevertheless valid) objection to the Jamesian viewpoint runs as follows: the reason that I know that someone committed an unjust act and the reason I become angry is not because I flush upon hearing about it. Rather, I am indignant (and may or may not flush with anger) in the encounter with a person's action, precisely because it is unjust (Bennett and Hacker 2003). The reason I know it is unjust is not because I detect bodily changes, but because I understand that the act tramples on someone's rights or is disrespectful. Anger as an emotion is *directed at* an object or event in the world (and not at changes in the organism). In other words, I have a *reason* to feel angry when someone acts unjustly.

Anger, like other emotions, is a normative response to an event, rather than a purely causal or mechanical reaction to changes in the body. This is not to say that the body is of no importance in our emotional lives – as discussed in the previous chapter – rather, the body is important because it is part of the individual's active way of *understanding the world*. It is through the body that I am open to a world that needs to be understood. However, bodily changes are not the primary object of emotional understanding. We have already seen that the most significant emotion theories in psychology – those that have stressed the intentional and normative nature of emotions – are the 'appraisal theories'. It is these theories that we must now integrate into an understanding of the extended mind.

If emotions are inherently intentional and normative (and hence have a cognitive component), the question is to what extent this depends upon the external scaffoldings provided by the environment. Returning to our initial vignette, we see that the emotion of grief is intimately connected to physical objects (a coffin, photos of the deceased, their belongings) and aesthetic practices (music and singing), as well as the socio-material form of the ceremony, the church as an institution and several other traditions for organising emotional life. We also know from ethnographic and cross-cultural studies that grief manifests itself differently in different cultures and eras (Kofod 2017; Rosenblatt 2001). Different cultures embody different sets of 'feeling rules' (Hochschild 1979) and 'emotionologies' (Gerrod Parrott and Harré 2001), i.e. socio-normative scripts for how to express emotions in specific contexts.

I would argue that our grief reactions – and the ensuing psychological and bodily experiences – are often dependent on material, social and semiotic mediators in the environment, which support (or 'scaffold') the emotions and can be considered part of them. The artefacts described in the vignette help direct the bereaved person's attention to their lost loved one and initiate a cycle of affective reminiscence. This is central to the emotion of grief – without it, it is difficult to imagine that such an emotion would be possible. Without these physical, aesthetic, ritualistic and institutional 'scaffolds' that help us remember our loved one and manifest our grief, we would at most be left with an amorphous physiognomic process, which would be insufficient to constitute the human emotion of grief as such. It is through these extended socio-material scaffoldings that we are able to identify feelings as instances of grief – we only recognise grief if we understand that we have lost a loved one. This understanding is best thought of as constituted by a range of scaffoldings and mediators, rather than as a subjective idea in the head of a lone individual. In the next section, I lend further support to this idea by discussing the affective niche that makes the human emotion of grief possible in a cultural ecology of emotion.

Grief's affective niche

One of the first attempts to apply the theory of the extended mind to emotions was Griffiths and Scarantino's (2009) article 'Emotions in the wild'. They argue that emotions should not be seen as primarily internal states in the organism (which would make them indistinguishable from simple sensations like itches or physical pains), but rather as social signals, culturally underpinned by social norms, which are designed to influence other organisms in certain contexts. Their theory points in two directions – emotions are something humans *undergo*, but they are also something we *actively* perform in our attempts to change the social environment (Attig (2011) describes grief in precisely these terms). Since this article was published, a small but significant group of scholars have continued to theorise on the extendedness of emotions. In his article on the subject, Krueger (2014) goes further than Griffiths and Scarantino, and articulates two versions of the extended mind hypothesis in relation to emotions: *the hypothesis of bodily extended emotions* and *the hypothesis of environmentally extended emotions*.

The idea that emotions are not just in the head, but are also bodily extended and embedded processes is without doubt the least controversial of these approaches. I touched upon it in the previous chapter when I introduced the phenomenology of the body as described by Merleau-Ponty and 'the grieving body' as analysed by

DuBose (1997) and others. While the body plays a role in James's and Damasio's emotion theories, as discussed above, it is only as one single element in a causal chain that leads to the emotion, which consists of the mind registering bodily changes. Unlike theories that approach emotions as some kind of inner mental phenomenon, the view of emotions as bodily extended phenomena claims that the body itself can be affected by the world's vicissitudes, and as such is central to the individual's emotional life. However, grief necessitates that the body and the person are involved in a *situation* in the world. In his *Philosophical Investigations*, Wittgenstein makes the following thought-provoking remarks about grief as a phenomenon:

> 'Grief' describes a pattern which recurs, with different variations in the weave of our life. If a man's bodily expression of sorrow and joy alternated, say with the ticking of a clock, here we should not have the characteristic formation of the pattern of sorrow or the pattern of joy.
>
> 'For a second he felt violent pain.' – Why does it sound queer to say: 'For a second he felt deep grief?' Only because it so seldom happens?
>
> But don't you feel grief *now*? ('But aren't you playing chess *now*?') The answer may be affirmative; but that does not make the concept of grief any more like the concept of a sensation. – The question was really, of course, a temporal and personal one, not the logical question which we wanted to raise. (1958: 174).

Here, Wittgenstein employs his usual, questioning, conversational and enigmatic style to examine the practical deployment of our concepts, in an attempt to burrow down to their meaning. The reason that it sounds strange to say that a person felt deep grief for a second is that grief is a temporal process – it follows a pattern, based on a context that Wittgenstein calls 'the weave of our life'. This is in contrast to pain, which is an immediate 'sense notion' that is, to a far greater extent, felt directly 'inside the body'. If it is true that grief's presence in our lives requires a background, a 'weave of life', then this Wittgensteinian comment takes us a step closer to a theory of grief as an extended phenomenon. Conversely, if the internalist theories of James and Damasio had been correct, it would make sense to say that someone felt deep grief for a second, regardless of the circumstances. The extract from Wittgenstein demonstrates, therefore, that grief is not an inner mental object, but an emotion that is manifested by a living human body that exists in both a temporal and an environmental context. In other words, in an *affective niche*. This brings us to Krueger's second hypothesis – the hypothesis of environmentally extended emotions.

Colombetti and Krueger define affective niches, quite broadly, as 'instances of organism-environment couplings (mutual influences) that enable the realisation of specific affective states' (Colombetti and Krueger 2015: 1160). In order to unpack this general definition, we will map the affective niche of grief by introducing two distinctions from the sparse literature on extended emotions. The first, as discussed by Slaby (2014), concerns a difference between *diachronic* and *synchronic* scaffolding. The term 'scaffolding' comes from socio-cultural theory, and simply means that a process is guided and supported by the social and/or material environment in which it unfolds (Griffiths and Scarantino 2009: 440). Diachronic scaffolding refers to how emotions are shaped 'by cultural frames, scripts, templates (and we should add: *institutions* of emotion such as romantic love [. . .])' (Slaby 2014: 40). This is related to other concepts introduced above, such as the culture's 'feeling rules' and 'emotionology'. In a more general discussion of the extended mind, Gallagher (2013) elaborates on the theme of cognitive extension by linking it to processes and social practices that occur within cultural institutions, which he calls 'mental institutions'. He defines mental institutions as ones that help us accomplish certain cognitive processes, or even constitute those processes, and in doing so illustrate how cognition can be socially extended. Gallagher mentions legal and educational systems as examples of mental institutions, and claims that 'these socially established institutions sometimes constitute, sometimes facilitate and sometimes impede but in each case enable and shape our cognitive interactions with other people' (2013: 7). The psychological process of reaching a verdict in a trial, for example, is unthinkable (in reality, meaningless) without the judicial system's scaffolding. Without a legal system, there would be no sentences. This is also true of our emotional interactions. Without normative and institutional scripts about what, how and when to feel, the individual in mourning would not know how to enact their emotional life. These scripts are not simply 'in the head', but manifest in the social practices of cultures, which change all the time.

Tony Walter charts the historical development of the culture of grief, along with the transformation in its emotional scripts. He thinks that grief 'is performed, evoked by social contexts as much as bursting out from within' (1999: 120). This is also one of the central ideas in this book: that grief is about both the experience of loss ('inside'), but also social and societal normativity ('outside'). Based on this (normative, intentional, appraisal-theory) understanding of grief, we see how the experience of grief is composed of different scripts that have evolved over the history of culture. As we saw in the book's introduction, the cultural preoccupation with grief emerged as a consequence of the secularisation and individuation processes that arose in the wake of modernity. Earlier religious concerns about the destiny of the deceased's soul in the afterlife were gradually replaced by a concern with the destiny of the bereaved, who must live on without their loved one. This involved strict mourning practices, which had been largely determined by how they served the deceased person's soul, gradually being replaced by a focus on the grieving process and how this aided the bereaved individual's return to the general life in society. The focus of memorials and monuments shifted from ensuring the deceased's salvation to helping the bereaved to express their grief (see, e.g. the *Angel of Grief*, discussed in Chapter 1).

More generally, Walter articulates seven diachronic scripts for modern grief: personal grief, anomic grief, private grief, forbidden grief, time-limited grief, distracted grief and expressive grief (1999: 152). I will not go into them in detail here, but the list illustrates that there is almost a menu of grief scripts that we can all use to find our own personal way of dealing with loss. Although originally viewed as liberating, the relaxing of the former, strictly regulated mourning practices has increasingly been criticised for leaving the individual mourner in a state of anomie (lacking social norms). Although no one would call for the imposition of rituals on bereaved individuals, this lack of agreed norms for grieving – and the problem of de-ritualisation, 'multi-ritualisation' or 'individually tailored rituals', as Walter terms it (1999: 131) – poses new challenges for bereaved individuals.

One example of a material artefact that has helped to create a micro-ecological affective niche for grief is the artist Itaru Sasaki's wind phone. The wind phone is in a white telephone box in the middle of Sasaki's garden, overlooking the water. Whoever picks it up hears only the babbling brook and the rustling of the wind. The phone is not connected to anything. It is in an old-fashioned telephone box that Sasaki installed in his garden in 2010 after his cousin died of cancer. He used the phone to talk to his cousin, as part of his grieving process. Since his words could not reach his cousin via a normal phone, he thought 'that they might be carried to him by the wind. It was a way to get the darkness to gradually disappear from the heart.'[15]

After the earthquake on 11 March 2011, the most powerful in Japan's history, people started coming to Sasaki's garden to use the phone. The earthquake also caused a tsunami and led to the nuclear disaster at Fukushima. More than 19,000 people died, and vast swathes of the local material culture were wiped out. People needed a place to go and express their grief. Many found their way to the wind phone, sometimes several hundred people a month, from all over Japan. A TV station made a documentary about the phone. The current mayor of the local town has said that he wants to use the wind phone as part of his own personal grieving process, but that he refuses to do so until he has fulfilled his duty to the local community. In Japan, the bones of the dead are of great importance in funeral practices. Mourners pluck bones from the ashes after the cremation and put them in an urn. However, many of those killed during the earthquake were never found, which rendered such practices impossible. That may be why so many bereaved people have sought solace in the wind phone, which in some way compensates for the absence of established rituals. It serves as a new ritual practice, one that is relatively independent of specific belief systems. The phone brings mourners to a natural landscape, overlooking the sea from which the tsunami descended, and which brings both life (in the form of food) and death. The wind phone is an interesting example of the human capacity to create an aesthetic practice for grief in the midst of a deeply tragic situation. It is possible that this practice will gain meaning in a diachronic perspective, and provide a material scaffolding for grief in the local cultural context.

This brings me to the second category – synchronous scaffolding. This is a more immediate 'shaping of emotional experience by direct coupling and continuous interaction with the environment' (Slaby 2014: 40). It is concerned with the concrete, the here-and-now, e.g. the mourner at the funeral, visiting the grave, looking at pictures, listening to a eulogy or a piece of music. We might also make a distinction between the *individual tools* that people use to feel emotions and *collective* forms of emotional scaffolding. These represent different aspects of the affective niche – some are constructed by the individual alone, others are only possible through collective action.

Examples of the former include how bereaved individuals organise their lives, for example creating an altar with photos and other symbols representing the dead loved one, getting a tattoo or wearing a piece of jewellery as a physical manifestation of the bond to the deceased. Examples from the collective category include songs and music in the church, which Krueger describes as follows: 'the mournful reverence and sub-dued dynamics of funeral music speaks – and, indeed, *shapes* – the collective grief (and its associated expres-sions) of those in attendance' (2014: 548). Krueger does not deny the first-person nature of emotions – that an individual feels the grief. Rather, his argument is that grief can be shared by more than one person. This may sound strange, but it is an example of an instance in which 'it takes two to tango' – some phenomena, by their very nature, can only be experienced collectively. This also opens up an understanding of practices of collective grief enacted by professional mourners in dif-ferent cultures, e.g. the traditional keeners of Ireland. In many situations in our lives, we recognise that it makes a difference to our experience whether we are alone or together with others (think of enjoying a concert or looking at a beautiful sunset). This is particularly true of emotions like grief. The patterns and rhythms of crying also differ depending on whether people are alone or not (Katz 1999). Likewise, silence experienced in solitude is qualitatively different from shared silence. While the former may often go unnoticed, the experi-ence of silence shared with others can have multiple connotations – it may feel awkward or safe, depending on the circumstances. In the literature on the subject, the silence surrounding death is often discussed as a problematic aspect of contemporary Western grief cultures (Doka 2016). In a culture that generally emphasises verbal and emotional expression, other people's silence regarding our loss may be considered hurtful and offensive. Conversely, bereaved individuals may feel a normative pressure to express grief in situations where they find doing so uncomfortable. In any case, the presence of other people qualitatively alters the experience and meaning of silence and grief.

Conclusion: What is to be gained by viewing grief as extended?

Throughout the twentieth century, grief has been subjected to individualised, universalised and psychologised analyses. In other words, it has been depicted as an intra-psychological, mental phenomenon, analytically distinct from socio-cultural and -material practices and technologies. However, recent work within the sociology of emotions, anthropology and the history of emotions challenges this conception of grief as a universal and ahistorical phenomenon (Scheer 2012; Scheper-Hughes 1993). In my view, the emerging literature on extended emotions offers a promising analytical framework for examining grief's affective niche. By expanding the scope of our psychological analyses from the individual mind to the embodied mind in its embedded/extended societal environment, the extended mind perspective allows us to explore how 'grief work' takes place not only in individual minds, but also between people, enabled and scaffolded by socio-material practices and technologies, i.e. an *ecology of grief*. This perspective can, for example, inspire future studies of the importance of socio-material grief practices such as online bereavement groups, home

altars, diaries, tattoos and individual or collective rituals. The desire for common rituals is often expressed in
people's descriptions of grief, as in the following excerpt
from Naja Marie Aidt's poetry:

> We wish people still wore mourning armbands the first
> year.
> We wish people still wore black the first year.
> We wish our mark could be visible so others could see
> our mark.
> We wish rituals still existed.
> So we make our own rituals. (2017: 143–4)

The practical consequences of this chapter's perspective on a grief ecology include critical examinations of
contemporary diagnostic procedures and intervention
methods concerning grief, as well as studies of how contemporary grief cultures both enable and restrict certain
ways of experiencing and enacting grief. The former
could lead to a broadening of current individualistic
approaches to diagnostics and interventions. This could
involve, e.g., applying relationally and materially sensi-
tive approaches to grief complications, or developing
community-oriented interventions that can supplement
the individual-oriented approach of contemporary
bereavement care (see the next chapter for an analysis
of the diagnostic approach to grief).

Prior to offering individual counselling to bereaved
people, more collective interventions might be envisaged,
such as providing opportunities for sharing experiences
and memories among those affected by a bereavement,
and developing collective rituals by which to remember
loved ones. Individualistic approaches are already being
challenged, especially at grassroots level, by bereave-

ment groups and collective remembrance rituals. A critical examination of the cultural and socio-material conditions for grieving also highlights how these conditions enable and restrict individual experiences and enactments of grief. For example, a potential first step toward challenging and altering the current conditions for grieving may be to address how the contemporary inclination to individualise grief leads to loneliness and isolation.

Overall, this chapter has sought to argue that grief is not just 'a feeling inside', but, as a complex psychological phenomenon, is co-constituted by both a social world (i.e. by other people, especially fellow mourners who take part in and share the emotion) and a material context, with all its artefacts, rituals and technologies. Grief is a cognitive emotion. Just as our cognition is extended and expanded, so too is grief. It takes place in an ecology of affective niches, in a way that is not just incidental but a fundamental dimension of our emotional life. Just as we use tools and technologies when we think about and solve problems (calculators, Post-it notes), so we also do when we engage emotionally in the world – like when we grieve the loss of a loved one.

6

Grief as a Psychiatric Diagnosis?

In recent years, one of the most high-profile topics of academic debate about grief has been the tendency toward medicalisation and pathologisation that has culminated in the psychiatric diagnoses for complicated grief. In the fifth edition of the American Psychiatric Association's *Diagnostic and Statistical Manual of Mental Disorders* (DSM), published in 2013, a new diagnosis for complicated grief (Persistent complex bereavement disorder) was included in the section 'Conditions for further study'. When the World Health Organization published the new edition of its classification system, the *ICD-11*, in 2018, it also included a new diagnosis called 'Prolonged grief disorder'.

In this chapter, I first briefly present the emerging diagnostic criteria for grief and discuss the emergence of psychiatric diagnoses in the context of what has been called the 'diagnostic culture' of contemporary society (Brinkmann and Petersen 2015). I also raise the question of the legitimacy of psychiatric diagnoses for complicated grief by discussing the diagnoses in the light of four general and widespread theories of mental disorders. I recommend a cautious approach, according to which grief should primarily be thought of as an existential condition that can lead to mental disorders, but not as a mental disorder per se. The fact that grief may make somebody ill is different from saying that it is a disease.

Psychiatric grief categories in a diagnostic culture

The term 'diagnostic culture' was developed as a general term to indicate that medical diagnoses, in particular psychiatric ones, are now used in many countries for multiple purposes that have little or nothing to do with traditional psychiatric practices (Brinkmann 2016a). Diagnostic terms such as depression, anxiety, autism and ADHD have become commonplace when we talk about our problems. They function as powerful categories in the social and health systems of modern welfare states, and they have entered media discourse and popular culture. The concepts of illness and disorder – and the diagnoses we employ to designate our problems – are no longer just medical, biological and psychological concepts, but also bureaucratic, social and administrative entities (Rosenberg 2007: 5). McGann goes so far as to conclude that 'diagnoses have become part of how we make sense of ourselves, each other, and the world' (2011: 343). This process has now been extended to cover grief as well.

The main catalysts for this spread of diagnoses are the diagnostic manuals. The first edition of the DSM was published in 1952. Although diagnostic terms were, of course, used before this time, it was only in the second half of the twentieth century that psychiatric diagnoses really started to spread from practices in clinics and hospitals to schools, welfare bodies and families. Most of us now use diagnostic terms such as depression, anxiety, bipolar, ADHD, PTSD and OCD, as well as quasi-diagnoses such as stress and burnout, when talking about the problems that we or our children face in everyday life. We read self-help books about how to manage various mental disorders that can perhaps be diagnosed, and consume novels and TV series (e.g. *The Sopranos*, *Homeland* or *The Bridge*) in which the heroes or villains suffer from diagnosable afflictions. It is this trend to which the concept of 'diagnostic culture' refers (Brinkmann 2017b). In 1952, when *DSM-I* appeared, there were 106 psychiatric diagnoses in a manual of 130 pages. In 1994, with *DSM-IV*, the number of diagnoses had increased to 297 in an 886-page manual (Williams 2009). Now, with the publication of *DSM-5* (the APA has changed to Arabic numerals), we see fifteen new diagnoses (including hoarding disorder and nicotine dependence), while a few others (most notably, Asperger's syndrome) have been removed. In other words, the number of official diagnoses soared dramatically in the latter half of the twentieth century. Including subcategories, there are now estimated to be a staggering 1,000 or so psychiatric diagnoses (Gjedde 2015).

As far as grief is concerned, two noteworthy changes occurred between *DSM-IV* and *DSM-5* (Parkes 2014; Wakefield 2013a). First, the 'bereavement exclusion' was removed from the diagnosis of major depression. *DSM-IV* had sought to avoid confusing grief with depression by making diagnosis of the latter difficult during the first two months after the loss of a loved one.

Many of the symptoms of grief and depression overlap, and so, in colloquial terms, a period of two months' grief was 'allowed' after a loss. A depression diagnosis could only be issued if the symptoms persisted after those initial two months. This exclusion probably contributed positively in terms of reducing cases of misdiagnosis, but critics argued that it also had negative effects, in that it 'deprived people of medical help and treatment during a period of maximum vulnerability, simply because they had been bereaved' (Parkes 2014: 114). Intuitively, it does seem problematic to deny people access to treatment for depression on the grounds that they are also suffering from grief.

However, the removal of the bereavement exclusion has also been met with a great deal of counter-criticism, including from the noted analyst of pathologisation Jerome Wakefield. He argues that the removal is 'invalid and empirically unsupported', and that it is wholly inadequate to replace the exclusion 'by a vague note stating that normal grief and reactions to other stressors can have depressive symptoms, and the clinician must judge the diagnosis, but with no grounding criteria' (2013a: 171). According to Horwitz and Wakefield, without the exclusion criterion, between half and a third of all bereaved people might be diagnosed as suffering from depression a month after a loss (2007: 31). There seems to be a genuine dilemma here. On the one hand, modern health services operate in accordance with the logic of diagnostic cultures, and issue diagnoses when patients have a sufficient number of symptoms (in this case, of depression) in order to facilitate treatment. On the other hand, there is a risk of a painful existential phenomenon such as grief being misdiagnosed as a mental disorder, which was the very reason for the bereavement exclusion in the first place. Another debate concerns the possibility that the proliferation of depression diagnoses could lead to the pathologisation of common human sadness (as discussed in detail by Horwitz and Wakefield 2007). This is something of a minefield, and beyond the focus of this book. I am aware that the current diagnosis of depression is problematic, especially in terms of the risk of over-diagnosis, but that is a separate and additional problem to the one with which I am concerned here: the distinction between depression and grief, and the problems inherent in the pathologisation of the latter.

This leads us to the other major change concerning grief in *DSM-5*. It introduces a whole new category, 'Persistent complex bereavement-related disorder', in the section 'Conditions for further study'. Prior to *DSM-5*, there was simply no psychiatric category that dealt with non-depressive feelings of grief. The new diagnostic criteria for 'Persistent complex bereavement-related disorder' consist of the following (Jordan and Litz 2014: 182):

(A) Death of a close other
(B) Since the death, at least one of the following on most days to a clinically significant degree for at least 12 months:
1. Persistent yearning for the deceased
2. Intense sorrow and emotional pain in response to the death
3. Preoccupation with the deceased
4. Preoccupation with the circumstances of the death
(C) Since the death, at least six of the following on most days to a clinically significant degree for at least 12 months after the death:

1. Marked difficulty accepting the death
2. Disbelief or emotional numbness over the loss
3. Difficulty with positive reminiscing about the deceased
4. Bitterness or anger related to the loss
5. Maladaptive appraisals about oneself in relation to the deceased or the death (e.g. self-blame)
6. Excessive avoidance of reminders of the loss
7. A desire to die to be with the deceased
8. Difficulty trusting other people since the death
9. Feeling alone or detached from other people since the death
10. Feeling that life is meaningless or empty without the deceased or the belief that one cannot function without the deceased
11. Confusion about one's role in life or a diminished sense of one's identity
12. Difficulty or reluctance to pursue interests or to plan for the future (e.g. friendships, activities) since the loss
(D) The disturbance causes clinically significant distress or impairment in social, occupational or other important areas of functioning
(E) The bereavement reaction must be out of proportion or inconsistent with cultural or religious norms.

Although Wakefield does not, in principle, reject adding 'a suitably formulated category for enduring intense grief without a normal trajectory of adaptation', he nevertheless criticises the actual diagnosis of 'persistent complex bereavement-related disorder' on the grounds that it represents a problematic compromise between competing theories of grief, and has 'high potential for abuse', with a potential for over-diagnosis and over-treatment (Wakefield 2013a: 172). The estimated prevalence of the condition is 2.4 to 4.8 per cent, and it is more common in women than men (Parkes

2014). However, if we only look at bereaved individuals, studies indicate that as many as 20 to 33 per cent may meet the criteria for complicated grief (Piper and Ogrodniczuk 2013). In other words, a very high number of bereaved people will potentially qualify for this diagnosis.

In terms of its theoretical basis, the DSM category is quite eclectic (in that it comprises four distinct elements). The proposed category of complicated grief in the WHO's ICD system seems to be more closely tied to a specific theory, namely the one put forward by Holly Prigerson (Prigerson et al. 2009; Prigerson and Maciejweski 2006). The WHO website provides the following definition of the diagnosis of 'Prolonged grief disorder':

> Prolonged grief disorder is a disturbance in which, following the death of a partner, parent, child, or other person close to the bereaved, there is persistent and pervasive grief response characterized by longing for the deceased or persistent preoccupation with the deceased accompanied by intense emotional pain (e.g. sadness, guilt, anger, denial, blame, difficulty accepting the death, feeling one has lost a part of one's self, an inability to experience positive mood, emotional numbness, difficulty in engaging with social or other activities). The grief response has persisted for an atypically long period of time following the loss (more than 6 months at a minimum) and clearly exceeds expected social, cultural or religious norms for the individual's culture and context. Grief reactions that have persisted for longer periods that are within a normative period of grieving given the person's cultural and religious context are viewed as normal bereavement responses and are not assigned a diagnosis. The disturbance causes significant impairment

in personal, family, social, educational, occupational or other important areas of functioning.[16]

These are not precise diagnostic criteria in list form, but looser descriptions of the way in which the diagnosis should be arrived at. Unlike the DSM category, the WHO makes explicit that even in cases where people grieve for longer periods of time than is considered normal in their cultural context, this does not in itself warrant a diagnosis. It is not simply the length of time that is decisive, but rather the impairment caused by 'the grief response'. However, the WHO description does assign a time frame – the symptoms persist six months after a loss, whereas the DSM category states that the symptoms should be present on most days for at least twelve months. From one perspective, it would appear likely that more people would be diagnosed under the DSM category, but from another, the reverse might be the case. Once *ICD-11* is finalised and in general use, researchers can begin to study the inter-diagnostic reliability of the two categories (for a comparison, see Jordan and Litz 2014, in which the authors express a clear preference for the ICD diagnosis).

These new diagnoses medicalise grief. We can draw a distinction between pathologisation, which is the process by which a painful phenomenon is turned into an illness or disorder, and medicalisation, which means framing a phenomenon in medical terms. As such, medicalisation is a value-neutral concept – it does not automatically imply that a phenomenon is *illegitimately* medicalised, even though most analyses of the topic are critical (Conrad 2007). Analyses of medicalisation typically focus on two aspects. First, how medical categories

Grief

are developed and applied to more and more phenomena all of the time; second, how people in modern society have internalised medical and diagnostic perspectives in their self-understanding (Conrad 2007: 14). The first aspect can be called 'medicalisation from above'; the second, 'medicalisation from below'. Grief, it seems, is undergoing medicalisation from both above and below at the same time. Psychiatrists, psychologists and various NGOs and treatment centres are all pushing for the introduction of diagnoses for complicated grief (from above). However, there is also evidence to suggest that some bereaved individuals are embracing their grief diagnosis (from below) (Kofod 2015).

Very few studies have been conducted of people's understandings of and attitudes to grief diagnoses. One exception is Kofod's (2015) study of how bereaved parents experience and express their grief after losing a young child. Based on qualitative interviews, the study identifies four main ways in which bereaved parents relate to the possibility of their grief being diagnosed:

(1) They use the diagnosis as a *legitimising practice*: There is tendency among bereaved parents to see a diagnosis as a possible legitimisation of their suffering. A grief diagnosis (which is not currently available in Denmark) would give them 'advantages' that may be emotional ('the right to grieve'), material (e.g. access to sick leave, economic and therapeutic support) and relational (since a diagnostic category might give them a legitimate way of communicating their suffering to others).

(2) Diagnosis as a *demarcation practice*: The majority of the participants interviewed believed that a grief diagnosis could be used to differentiate between normal or

158

natural grief reactions on the one hand and pathological or dysfunctional reactions on the other.

(3) Diagnosis as (illegitimate) *pathologisation*: This perspective rejects the pathologisation of grief, and maintains that even intense and long-lasting grief should be seen as a variation of a normal reaction to profound loss. A small number of Kofod's interviewees shared this view, but just one person expressed the final perspective:

(4) Diagnosis as a *normative ideal*: This represents an intriguing challenge to the widely held notion of psychiatric diagnoses as stigmatising. One participant stated that, given the existence of a grief diagnosis, she would feel an urge to 'live up to' the criteria in order to prove to herself (and others) that she loved her dead child sufficiently. She says that if she was not diagnosed as suffering from grief, she would ask herself whether she was 'grieving enough' for her child.

In the next few years, once grief diagnoses have been rolled out in health services in the welfare states, it will be important for researchers in the human and social sciences to analyse the problems and potentials associated with the increasing medicalisation of grief. Summing up the existing literature on the topic, Bandini (2015) articulates three major consequences of these developments in diagnostic practice. First, removing the bereavement exclusion from the depression diagnosis (which I discussed above) may lead to over-diagnosis and over-treatment of grief as depression. Second, there is now an increasing potential for the pharmaceutical industry to market treatments for complicated grief. Indeed, medical trials have already been conducted in this area (Jordan and Litz 2014). Preliminary results from trials of antidepressants as a treatment for complicated grief suggest that the medicine has a beneficial effect, especially in combination with psychotherapy (Shear et al. 2016). Third, the introduction of a psychiatric approach calls into question traditional cultural practices of dealing with grief (Bandini 2015: 347). What happens to the existing ways of helping the bereaved when their grief becomes a psychiatric diagnosis and a matter for the health service? Some would argue that the existing ways of helping are problematic – or, indeed, conspicuous by their absence. If that is the case, then surely diagnosis and psychiatric treatment are better than nothing? The answers to such questions depend largely on whether or not it is appropriate to diagnose any kind of grief, no matter how intense, as a mental disorder. This is discussed in the next section, in which I refer to four general perspectives on what constitutes a mental illness or disorder.

What is a mental disorder?

Those who develop new diagnostic categories and treatments rarely tackle the most difficult yet fundamental question: what is a mental disorder? In his extremely thorough book on the subject, Derek Bolton, a leading authority in psychopathology, shows that we are a long way from being able to definitively answer this question. Bolton concludes that: 'There is, as far as I can see, no stable reality or concept of mental disorder; it breaks up into many, quite different kinds, some reminiscent of an old idea of madness or mental illness, others nothing like this at all' (2008: viii).

Bolton emphasises the heterogeneity of what is conventionally called mental disorder. This indicates that although some diagnostic categories may refer to genuine illnesses that are best understood as brain disorders (e.g. schizophrenia and bipolar disorder – although this is contested), others may be very different. Perhaps we should not expect that one particular approach to mental disorders will be able to cover them all. Nick Haslam has argued that:

> there is little reason to believe that any one of [the] accounts of the structure of psychiatric kinds is most adequate across the board. Instead, different accounts may suit different disorders. Some psychiatric conditions may be well described by the disease model, others by dimensional models, others by prototype models, and so on. (2014: 13)

There may even be reason to believe that certain mental 'disorders' are *not* disorders at all, but in fact ordinary human behaviours and reactions that are only to be expected under the circumstances. Examples might include 'everyday sorrows', which can be (mis-) interpreted as depression (Williams 2009); shyness, which might be pathologised as social phobia (Lane 2007); and perhaps unruly and inattentive behaviour, which some may see as cases of ADHD (Brinkmann 2014a). Nonetheless, it is worth looking at the suggested grief diagnoses in the light of some influential theories of mental disorder. While there are many to choose from, I believe that the theories of Boorse and Wakefield and of phenomenologists like Jaspers and Bolton are the key ones. They can be called naturalist theory, harmful dysfunction theory, phenomenological theory and nominalist theory, respectively (Brinkmann 2016a).

Grief

The naturalist theory

The naturalist theory claims that illness in general is simply a name for subnormal functioning relative to natural levels. This classic theory has been particularly strongly advocated by Christopher Boorse. The aim is to provide a value-neutral understanding of illness and health by defining disease as an internal state of the organism that interferes with the performance of a natural function of the species (Boorse 1976: 62). A *mental* disorder, therefore, is defined specifically as a statistical abnormality in one or more psychological functions. In the case of grief, there is a substantial tradition among scholars of approaching the phenomenon within an evolutionary framework. Earlier in this book, we looked at Bowlby's ethological theory of grief and attachment, and Parkes (1972) offers a later example. Bowlby's highly influential theory outlined four phases of grief (numbness and disbelief; yearning and searching; disorganisation and despair; reorganisation), but these have not been well supported by subsequent empirical research (Archer 1999). The more general link between attachment and grief has fared better from an evolutionary perspective, as the grief reaction can be seen either (as Bowlby argued) as an evolved response to separation or (as Parkes argued) as the 'cost of commitment' for creatures who are attracted to and bound by other creatures of the same species (Parkes 1972: 64). In the latter case, it is not grief per se that evolved, but rather commitments and attachments between individuals, in relation to which grief is seen as an evolutionary 'by-product', as also discussed earlier.

However, there are two further questions regarding the naturalist theory and grief as a possible mental disorder: does the theory warrant the conceptualisation of some forms of grief as a mental disorder? And is the theory itself a valid approach to mental disorder? Regarding the first question, the answer seems to be yes. If grief becomes intense and deviant enough that the bereaved individual is incapable of functioning to an acceptable degree (which remains to be specified, of course), then the theory states that the person is suffering from a mental disorder – just as they would be diagnosed as suffering from heart disease if not enough blood circulated through their veins to facilitate normal functioning. A more serious problem afflicts the second question. It remains rather unclear, especially when we consider mental disorders, what precisely constitutes a 'natural function'. For humans, it is surely 'natural' to be cultural, and around the world there is great cultural diversity – and therefore many divergent norms – concerning normality and disorder (Shweder 2008). In addition, some conditions (e.g. mouth diseases like caries) are so prevalent as to be statistically normal, but this does not disqualify them as actual illnesses.

This theory seems too simple and problematic. Bolton (2008: 113) mentions three of the main problems. First, it is assumed that a deviation from a statistical norm implies problems in terms of function, which may – but need not – be the case. In the case of grief, for example, we know that some elderly people 'have no intention of "getting over it", and are actually looking forward to joining their dead husband or wife shortly' (Walter 1999: 47). While this represents a deviation from the norm, it seems unreasonable to conclude that it means these people are suffering from a mental disorder. Second, when it comes to deviance, it is unclear where to draw the line between normality and disorder (e.g. one, two or three standard deviations below the mean?). This question becomes relevant when formulating the exact diagnostic criteria for a new mental disorder such as complicated grief: how many 'symptoms' and for how long? Third, statistical normality is always seen in relation to a population, but the theory does not specify which human population constitutes the benchmark relative to which people can be said to suffer from a mental disorder. This brings us back to the key point that the naturalist theory simply does not take sufficient account of cultural variation. In short, I believe that this theory is inadequate on its own terms. It has quite rightly been subjected to severe criticism over the years, and is therefore of no help when it comes to classifying grief as a mental disorder.

The harmful dysfunction theory

Next, we have Wakefield's (1992) influential theory of mental disorder as *harmful dysfunction*. This builds on the naturalist theory, but adds a crucial *value component* that substantially improves on naturalism. According to Wakefield, a state is a mental disorder if (a) it arises because of the failure (or dysfunction) of a naturally evolved psychological mechanism that (b) affects the person in a destructive (or harmful) way. Mental disorders are therefore harmful dysfunctions. As Wakefield makes clear, the second condition implies a value judgement, since something can be judged harmful in relation to the norms of a person's culture (the 'local moral order'). An interesting consequence of this theory is that many of the disorders currently listed in the DSM and ICD diagnostic systems would *not* be considered genuine disorders. For example, although it is experienced as harmful, common depression is usually *not* the result of a malfunctioning psychological mechanism, but more often the result of social conditions that exceed the individual's capacity to cope, causing stress, exhaustion and sadness (Horwitz and Wakefield 2005). According to Wakefield, classifying most instances of common depression as a mental disorder is unwarranted.

Again, we can ask two questions: what does the theory say about complicated grief as a mental disorder? How does it fare as a theory of mental disorder on its own terms? Wakefield provides an answer to the first question. He has persistently criticised one of the most common arguments for grief as a mental disorder, namely that complicated grief has a statistical correlation with negative outcomes later in life (Prigerson and Maciejweski 2006). Wakefield responds that this is a grossly invalid inference, and the fact that individuals who grieve more intensely than others have a higher risk of negative health outcomes later in life no more implies that their grief is a disorder 'than does the fact that there are heightened risks with pregnancy imply that pregnancy itself is a disorder' (2013b: 107). For something to count as a mental disorder, it must involve more than just a risk of harm and suffering. If not, all kinds of social suffering will be seen as instances of psychopathology, and that would entail an unwarranted pathologisation of people's life circumstances.

The question, then, is whether there is an inner 'grief mechanism', i.e. a mental module adapted by evolution, that can malfunction and cause distress. According to Wakefield's theory, this must be the case in order to justify a psychiatric diagnosis of grief. However, it is very difficult to assess. According to prevailing theories of grief based on evolutionary theory, it is not grief in itself that has adaptive value, but rather the affective bonds, the breaking of which results in grief. Archer concludes that 'grief (which is itself not adaptive) arises as a by-product of the broadly similar reaction to separation (which is adaptive)' (1999: 5). While there could in principle be dysfunction in a naturally evolved grief response, Wakefield denies that this has been identified by the suggested diagnostic criteria for complicated grief. He concludes that, as yet, we have no reason to think of grief as a potential mental disorder (Wakefield 2013b).

The second question – regarding harmful dysfunction theory itself – leads to the same main problem as the naturalist theory. It seems quite impossible to separate cultural functions from natural ones, and from conditions in human lives, in order to isolate 'naturally evolved psychological mechanisms', since most – if not all – higher mental functions depend on socialisation and culture (Vygotsky 1978). As Bolton says, it is doubtful whether 'there is a clear (enough) division between psychological functioning that is natural (evolved and innate), as opposed to social (cultivated)' (2008: 124). I will leave this discussion here, but conclude that the theory of mental disorder as harmful dysfunction is based on quite speculative conclusions from evolutionary psychology. As such, it is vulnerable to all sorts of challenges about which mental modules might be said to have evolved (if it is scientifically legitimate to talk about mental modules at all; see the critique of evolutionary biology in Sterelny 2012). Note that my objections here should not be understood as a rejection of the theory of evolution and Darwinism in general.

Rather, they question an evolutionary psychology that postulates the existence of discrete mental modules that supposedly emerged in the early stages of human evolution (see Chapter 3).

The phenomenological theory

Phenomenological theory can be traced back to Jaspers' (1997) classic work. While there is significant variation between the different phenomenological perspectives on mental disorder, what they have in common is the view that mental disorders break down the meaningful connections and relations in our mental lives, albeit without necessarily specifying the causes of these breakdowns. It is this focus on the experience rather than the underlying cause of the disorder that makes the theories phenomenological. In other words, if there is no meaningful connection between what *happens* and how a person *reacts* (e.g. between a non-dangerous situation and anxiety), and if the person's reaction is painful and lasting, then it seems relevant to talk about a mental disorder (regardless of whether the lack of connection stems from a dysfunctional 'psychological mechanism', defective neurological processes or some other factor).

This theory may at first glance hold the greatest promise (perhaps because of its lack of specificity). However, it would make it difficult to conceive of grief as a mental disorder, because grief, unlike depression, is *by definition* an expression of a meaningful connection with the deceased. This has been a major theme in this book, and is reinforced by the many maxims about grief that reflect this phenomenological perspective. For example, 'grief is the price of love' points to the fact that although grief can be intense and long-lasting, it still has phenomenological

meaning and significance. According to the phenomenological theory, grief would only be a potential mental
disorder in cases in which an individual experienced the
emotional response associated with grief but had in fact
suffered no loss. In such a situation, the meaningful connection would be missing. However, this is also logically
impossible, because grief without loss is what we would
call depression. The usefulness and adequacy of a phenomenological approach to mental disorder is open to
question (perhaps the theory is simply too general), but
accepting it makes it very difficult to articulate a valid
diagnostic category for complicated grief. From a phenomenological perspective, the checklist symptoms do
not indicate meaninglessness, rather very intense – but
still meaningful – grief reactions.

The nominalist theory

In his book on mental disorder, Bolton covers the three
competing theories above (as well as the neurological
theory, which I have omitted because it is less relevant
to grief), and concludes that none of them are satisfactory as general theories of mental disorder (although
he does not discuss them in relation to grief specifically). He argues that the naturalist theory and the
harmful dysfunction theory are inadequate, albeit for
different reasons, while the broader phenomenological
theory might be fine as such, but it does not address the
cause of the disorders. It also has the (in Bolton's eyes)
unfortunate consequence of suggesting that there is no
meaning in mental disorder (precisely because disorders
are defined as a breakdown and absence of meaning).
Bolton ends up rejecting all attempts to formulate an
essentialist theory that looks for the necessary and suf-

ficient conditions to call something a mental disorder. He argues that 'there is nothing intrinsic in particular biopsychological processes that makes them pathological, it is only their consequences, only if they persistently result in more harm than good' (2008: 205). His argument is that it is not the nature of people's problems that define them as psychiatric, social, moral, existential, etc. Rather, it is our systemic *response* to those problems.

While Bolton himself does not refer to his theory as nominalist, I have chosen to do so in this context because the term indicates that it is the very practice of categorising something in a given way that justifies its categorisation. There are no inherent properties in the various psychological states that tell us how to draw the line between pathology and normality. Only our practices of diagnosis and treatment do this. If no essentialist theory of mental disorder is valid, then perhaps we should follow Bolton and simply focus on psychiatry's purpose as being to help people in distress – without first defining whether we should think of distress in terms of mental disorder or from some other perspective. In effect, grief would be a mental disorder simply by virtue of being included in our diagnostic systems and treatment practices (which is what is currently happening). Nominalism means that if people turn to the system with complaints about suffering caused by loss, then the system treats their condition as a mental disorder. It is a disorder if people define it as such.

In the final analysis, however, I find this unsatisfactory, as the theory rests on an obviously circular argument. It ignores the fact that we (and here I refer not only to scientists, but also to treatment systems and patients in general) want to know *how* to approach people's problems. We want to know, for example, whether they are psychiatric or social, so we can avoid treating the consequences of poverty and social injustice as if they were psychiatric problems rather than political ones. We need some guidelines *before* we act. Bolton's nominalist alternative to the essentialist theories seems to be that whether something is a disorder or not – and therefore how we should respond to it – is in the eye of the beholder. This quickly leads to a social constructionist problematisation of the very idea of mental disorder. It implies that we could simply choose *not* to react to the problem as a mental disorder – but would that eliminate the problem in any meaningful sense? I would contend that this is not only simplistic, but disregards people's experiences of suffering.

Discussion

I have now reviewed four of the most important contemporary theories on mental disorder and tried to apply their definitions to the suggested diagnostic categories for complicated grief. For each one, I have asked how it would account for the possibility of such a diagnosis. I have also provided brief evaluations of how these theories of mental disorder might function in practice.

According to the naturalist theory, which states that mental disorder represents a statistically abnormal function, it is in principle possible that complicated grief could be a mental disorder. This would require a specification of what counts as a statistical sub-function, which is exactly what the different diagnostic criteria do. However, I have also argued that the theory itself is inadequate as a theory of mental disorder and *also* of grief as a possible mental disorder. Wakefield rightly points out that 'it is plainly a fallacy to identify statistical deviance with disorder'. He states that what is called complicated grief is just 'the upper end of the severity continuum of normal grief' (2013b: 102). Wakefield's own influential theory of mental disorder – the harmful dysfunction theory – generally fares much better because it operates with both a factual component (a possible dysfunction in an evolved psychological module) and a value component (concerning the level of harm). Its central problem, however, is that it appears to presuppose the possibility of separating what has naturally evolved from what has been culturally acquired, in a way that has been seriously questioned by recent advances in evolutionary theory (Sterelny 2012). Nevertheless, if we consider the theory as valid for the sake of the argument, it leads to the conclusion – underlined by Wakefield himself – that we have as yet no reason to think that complicated grief represents a mental disorder. In fact, he argues that the DSM's diagnostic criteria for complicated grief fail to discriminate disorder from intense normal grief, and are therefore likely to yield massive false-positive diagnoses. Wakefield (2012) recommends that the diagnosis be withdrawn. This has obviously not happened, and we must now await the phasing in of *ICD-11*, and yet another grief diagnosis.

The third theory of mental disorder I reviewed was the phenomenological theory. This does not consider the underlying causes of disorder, but focuses instead on the experience of a breakdown in meaningful connections in the individual's lifeworld, which the theory considers the defining characteristic of mental disorders in general.

171

While I am highly supportive of the phenomenological perspective – indeed, it forms the basis for this book – this theory of mental disorder has a certain weakness in that its generality threatens to make it empty, and perhaps too self-evident. It also seems to lead inevitably to the conclusion that complicated grief cannot be a disorder, given that grief – no matter how intense – is by definition a deeply meaningful response to loss.

Finally, I looked at Bolton's nominalist theory, which is effectively based on the indefinability of mental disorder. It states that whatever the psychiatric system diagnoses as human suffering in need of treatment should be considered a mental disorder, precisely because of this categorisation. Hence the nominalist aspect – it is the actual act of naming something within a treatment system that constitutes the disorder per se. From this perspective, complicated grief becomes a psychiatric disorder the moment that official bodies choose to define it as such. However, this means that theory becomes a precondition for whatever it seeks to explain (namely what a mental disorder is), which makes it difficult, if not impossible, to discuss whether some forms of medicalisation and pathologisation may be illegitimate. The risk of illegitimate pathologisation is, of course, the main reason why we discuss the validity of any diagnostic category, including grief as a possible mental disorder. While Bolton's approach is presented here as a nominalist theory of mental disorder, it is probably more correct to view it as a framework within the sociology of knowledge, one that takes an interest in classification practices in human institutions (Bowker and Star 2000). This means that this approach is only useful on a descriptive level. Instead, what is called for in this chapter – and by grief scientists in general – is a normative demarcation between ordinary forms of human suffering on the one hand, and pathological disorders and disturbances on the other.

One argument in support of Bolton's theory – and of the legitimacy of a complicated grief diagnosis in general – might be that some conditions (e.g. intense grief) can be successfully treated with either psychopharmaceuticals or psychotherapy, which proves that they are mental disorders. This argument is often heard in relation to other diagnoses such as ADHD, where people sometimes claim that the proof that it is a 'real' mental disorder is that the symptoms can be treated with a drug (e.g. methylphenidate in the case of ADHD) (Brinkmann 2016a). However, this argument is highly problematic, since the drug in question is likely to improve anyone's ability to focus, not only those diagnosed with ADHD. Secondly, and more generally, it is clearly a fallacy to conclude that because a certain intervention helps alleviate some painful condition, that condition is necessarily a disorder. Psychotherapy, for example, can be beneficial in relation to all sorts of psychological and existential problems, but that does not mean that these problems are mental disorders per se.

This brings us to the core dilemma of this chapter. Let us assume that Wakefield and other critics of pathologisation are right, and there is currently no satisfactory theory of mental disorder that backs the psychiatric diagnosis of complicated grief. In that case, should we follow Bolton's nominalist, pragmatic route, and say that the mere fact of people experiencing intense distress after a loss is sufficient to warrant a clinical diagnosis of complicated grief? This is a difficult question to answer. On the one hand, it is certainly true that a substantial number of bereaved individuals suffer in quite a problematic way, and it would be inhumane for a modern welfare society to refuse to help them. On the other hand, there is likely to be a significant cost involved in 'giving grief away' to the psychiatric system, and in doing so contributing to the further medicalisation and pathologisation of the phenomenon. Such a cost would not only be economic – it would primarily concern what Horwitz and Wakefield (2007) have called 'the loss of sadness' in modern society. By thinking of all kinds of sadness as pathological – provided that they are intense enough – we risk losing touch with the existential basis of human life. We risk supporting a hyper-efficient and individualist society that diagnoses ever increasing numbers of cases of suffering on the grounds that they make people slow and unproductive. This is one of the key issues in contemporary diagnostic culture (Brinkmann 2016a).

After reflecting on the pros and cons of a psychiatric grief diagnosis, my own cautious conclusion is to recognise that a modern welfare state ought to provide help for people in severe distress caused by bereavement, but that it might be fruitful to consider doing so *without* pathologising grief by including it in the psychiatric system. Before introducing a diagnosis for complicated grief, it might be worthwhile discussing other options for help that would seek to keep the phenomenon out of the hands of the psychiatric system (after all, the welfare state addresses other problems without first assigning them a psychiatric diagnosis). This chapter represents an initial attempt to consider if and how grief can be seen as a mental disorder. We must keep our minds open to the possibility that an understanding of complicated grief may be articulated based on a valid theory of mental disorder. However, I agree with Wakefield that we have not yet reached such an understanding, and that it would be wise to be cautious – to wait, reflect and conduct more empirical and theoretical research, before introducing a psychiatric grief diagnosis.

Conclusions

This chapter has interpreted the rise of psychiatric grief diagnoses in the context of contemporary diagnostic cultures. I have discussed the potential diagnoses in the light of four general theories of mental disorder. I concluded that no satisfactory theory has so far been articulated that warrants the formulation and introduction of complicated grief as a psychiatric diagnosis. At the moment, therefore, it is not legitimate to say, from a normative point of view, that grief can be a mental disorder or illness. On the other hand, it is certainly possible that grief can lead to recognised mental disorders, such as depression, which should be diagnosed and treated. For that reason, I think that people suffering from intense and prolonged grief should be acknowledged and helped. However, it would probably be preferable to do so without pathologising grief itself. A key question for future studies should be if and how well grieving individuals can be helped without a psychiatric diagnosis (perhaps for depression). In all likelihood, we will in the future see the introduction of psychiatric grief diagnoses, and therefore, as a complement to the present theoretical study, empirical research will be required to document the benefits and pitfalls of this development.

7

A Homeless Love

Grief may well be the oldest human emotion on record. Archaeological finds suggest that the Neanderthals engaged in ritual burial practices more than 60,000 years ago (Archer 1999: 55). Since then, all known human cultures have had specific ways of dealing with death, which clearly indicates that a human corpse is not considered just another inanimate object to be cast aside and discarded as waste, but is in some sense an individual with a certain degree of dignity.

According to the philosopher Michel Serres, human society begins when someone marks death symbolically, using physical symbols – which he calls 'statues' in the broad sense (Serres 2015). Human cultures and civilisations have always invested time and resources in graves and monuments to the dead. Denmark, where I come from, has more than 25,000 preserved burial mounds from the Stone, Bronze and Iron ages. Elsewhere in the world we encounter mausoleums and pyramids – places that for some cultures have acted as focal points for a whole civilisation's economy and social life. While this material evidence of death's anthropological significance does not directly describe grief, it does so indirectly. Grief is the individual's psychological bond with the dead, while memorials are society's collective bonds (Brescó and Wagoner, not yet published). There is no clear boundary between the individual and the collective, and even a modest tombstone in a cemetery is, for the bereaved, a kind of material marker of a person's life and death. While the primary purpose of pyramids and burial mounds – not to mention the 15,000-strong Terracotta Army guarding the body of China's first emperor – was to protect the dead in the afterlife, the gravestones and memorials of secular societies are primarily there to help the bereaved cope with their grief. In both cases, they are a way of integrating the dead into the lives of those left behind. All societies have a need to construct forefathers (and -mothers) in order to forge a link with the past that gives the living a self-understanding and sense of belonging. Grief offers substantial psychological material with which to forge these links. As the sociologist Tony Walter put it: 'grief underlies the very constitution of society' (1999: xvi).

This brings us to the central point of this book. If grief is fundamental and constitutive for human society – because social life basically entails guarding against and dealing with death and grief (Seale 1998) – then it is suddenly transformed from just one psychological phenomenon among many, to a key we need to unlock the deeper layers of the self and society. The fundamental thesis of this book is that grief says something crucial about both the human self – because it is a foundational emotion at the intersection between love and death – and about human society. Grief includes both existential invariants, because our relationship with finitude and death is inevitable, and some cultural and historical variations. While this book has primarily sought to identify the phenomenology of grief and its general psychology, it has also looked at how it has changed over time. In the previous chapter, the current transformations in manifestations of grief were linked to the emerging diagnostic culture. In my opinion, this dimension warrants a separate, more thorough and empirically grounded study. Is the current tendency toward pathologisation related to aspects of our society that exhort us to resist grief, with its sadness, contemplation and lack of utility? Our era is epitomised by a cult-like worship of various traits typically associated with childhood and youth (energy, outdoing ourselves, doing whatever we want, taking risks) (see, e.g. Barber 2007). Grief, on the other hand, can make us slow and backward-looking. It represents ties to the past rather than a vision of the future. Walter writes that a culture that looks backward will be more inclined to take its ties to the dead seriously (1999: 112). Our age is, in the opinion of several observers, characterised by an imperative toward happiness and positivity (Davies 2015), whereas grief is inherently heavy and sad, out of sync with society's demands to be agile, flexible and adaptable. Our age is also marked by a utilitarianism, in which we are required to 'make the most of it' (Brinkmann 2016c). But grief is way beyond any mere utilitarian calculation. It is not about achieving something or asking: 'what's in it for me?' Grief is just *there* – it is a pervasive, embodied recognition of loss and homeless love.

Although it is clear that grief is almost incompatible with society's demands for the ideal human, there is, of course, no deterministic link between that clash and the ongoing pathologisation of grief. However, it is right to bear those demands in mind as we seek to understand the current impetus to make complicated grief the subject of a psychiatric diagnosis. Are the diagnoses for complicated grief society's way of dealing with the inability of bereaved people to function properly (relative to social norms for work and productivity)? I think that is a question worth exploring as diagnostic thinking encroaches upon grief. We also need to discuss whether the individualisation that many social scientists have described as the hallmark of our time (e.g. Beck 2001) leaves the bereaved more isolated in their grief, at the risk of exacerbating the loneliness felt after a loss.

In an individualised society, we are expected (to use the sociologist Ulrich Beck's term) to find 'biographical solutions' for wider problems, solutions that we cobble together in our own lives. How are bereaved people meant to do this if we accept the premise that they need social support and a sense of community? Grief is not something that can ever be 'fixed', but being supported by others appears to be the diametrical opposite of a biographical solution. In the face of life's great existential dramas, modern human beings find it difficult to admit that they are powerless and dependent on others. When times are tough, therefore, there is a tendency to turn to psychiatric diagnostic thinking. If I cannot cope, is it because I am ill? Or is it because the situation I face *cannot* be coped with by anybody in isolation, but needs to be addressed collectively? A bereaved person who is sick with grief might just as well be ill due to loneliness. Perhaps, then, we should do something about loneliness, rather than merely focusing on diagnosing and treating grief?

Hopefully it has become clear that I am interested in grief both as a significant phenomenon in its own right and because it tells us something important about the human self and society. Of course, there are many themes related to grief that I have only touched on in passing – not least, the therapeutic treatment of intense and prolonged grief, religious and psychotherapeutic perspectives, studies of typical grief for specific groups (e.g. in relation to age, gender, ethnicity or religion), the importance of the specific nature of the loss for the grief experience (there are certainly big differences between losing a child, a spouse, a parent or a friend), and many more. The book has employed phenomeno-logical thinking that sees grief as involving a loss of a system of opportunities. This says something about the self (Chapter 2 on foundational emotions), the norma-tivity of psychological phenomena (Chapter 3 on the phenomenology of grief), feelings rooted in the body (Chapter 4 on the body in grief), and the importance of surroundings and environment (Chapter 5 on the ecol-ogy of grief).

I could also have covered the broader concept of *cultural* grief, which is the subject of increasing debate. This refers to the loss not only of *individual* systems of opportunities, but also of a *collective* system of meaning – and, in the final analysis, of a whole cultural world. The philosopher Jonathan Lear (2006), for example, delivered a moving analysis of the Crow Nation in North America, which collapsed and vanished when the Christian settlers took the land, killed the buffalo and set up reservations for the indigenous population. Within a few years, the Crow had lost their meaningful world. It was no longer possible to win honour by waging war against other tribes, former hierarchies disappeared, and traditional qualitative distinctions between good and bad no longer applied. The last principal chief (leader among leaders) of the Crow Nation, Plenty Coups, who died in 1932, told the story of the loss of the Crow cultural world, but also introduced a 'radical hope' (Lear's concept) that a new Crow culture would emerge that could give meaning and value to the people. Lear concludes that, to a certain extent, this has happened. I finish with this because it is human to search for hope in the midst of grief. However, I also mention it because Lear points to a cultural dimension of grief that deserves further study – not least because several cultural worlds look set to be obliterated in the not too distant future as a consequence of global (climate) change. Maybe one of those worlds will be our own, at least as we know it. My hope is that identifying the general nature of grief and its phenomenology will provide a useful basis for more specific studies, both those undertaken by our current research project 'The Culture of Grief', and those of other projects that are already under way.

Notes

1 See Sofie Sørensen, 'Vi befinder os i sorgens århun-drede', *Politiken*, 14 April 2017, at https://politiken.dk/kultur/art5912012/Vi-befinder-os-i-sorgens-%C3%A5rhundrede.

2 In this context, I understand ontology as the part of philosophy that deals with the basic ways in which some-thing can exist (or not).

3 This poem was translated into English by Susanna Nied and is available at: http://www.soerenulrikthomsen.dk/sut/translations/english/ShakenMirror.pdf.

4 Quotes in Stearns and Knapp 1996: 136.

5 See Kerrigan 2007 for a comprehensive and richly illus-trated monograph on the subject.

6 This chapter is based on my article 'The grieving animal: Grief as a foundational emotion', published in the journal *Theory & Psychology*.

7 It is relevant to mention that I use the term 'affective' as a generic term for feelings, emotions, moods and short-term states of shock. It refers to everything that *touches us*. Additionally, it is often relevant to distinguish between feelings and emotions. The former can refer both to sensations in the body (e.g. 'I have lost feeling in my

182

finger' or 'I can feel the rough surface of the tree') and to prolonged mental states. Psychologists often call such states emotions, and they are not located in the body in the same way as sensations. Joy, pride, anger or sadness have characteristic physical expressions, but we cannot say that we feel joy or anger in the arm or leg. This is because emotions are directed toward objects in the world, and represent ways of understanding the world. However, in an effort to avoid unnecessary jargon, I use the term 'feeling' to refer to what psychologists often call emotions. In other words, when talking about feelings, I do not mean sensations or immediate perceptions, but emotions. The following chapters will gradually develop a comprehensive emotion theory, in which grief is the focal point.

8 *Black Mirror* is a television series with a different story and cast in each episode. Common to all of the episodes is an interest in the consequences of new technology, in particular the many screens that surround us (phones, tablets, TVs), and in which we see ourselves in various ways. Hence the name *Black Mirror*.

9 For a recent exception, see Fuchs 2018, and several of the other sources cited in the previous chapter. This chapter is based on my English-language article 'The body in grief' in the journal *Mortality*.

10 See Cari Romm, 'Understanding how health weakens the body', *The Atlantic*, 11 September 2014, at https://www. theatlantic.com/health/archive/2014/09/understanding-how-grief-weakens-the-body/380006.

11 See Tom Gray, 'Your health and grief', PsychCentral, 8 October 2018, at https://psychcentral.com/lib/your-health-and-grief.

12 This chapter is based on the English-language article 'Grief as an extended emotion' published in *Culture & Psychology* and co-authored by Ester Holte Kofod. I

would like to thank Ester for allowing me to use the ideas from the article, as reworked in this chapter.

13 This chapter is based on the author's background in a Protestant Christian culture. It is worth remembering that the practices relating to death, funerals and grief vary greatly around the world (for an overview, see e.g. Parkes, Laungani and Young 2015).

14 Note that, in this context, the ecology concept is not about sustainability, but about the whole relationship between organisms and their environments.

15 Quoted from an article in *Politiken* by Sandra Brovall, 6 January 2018.

16 See ICD-11, '6B42 Prolonged grief disorder', at https://icd.who.int/dev11/l-m/en#/http%3a%2f%2fid.who.int%2ficd%2fentity%2f1183832314.

Bibliography

Aidt, N.M. (2017). *Har døden taget noget fra dig så giv det tilbage: Carls bog*. Copenhagen: Gyldendal.

Archer, J. (1999). *The Nature of Grief: The Evolution and Psychology of Reactions to Loss*. London: Routledge.

Ariès, P. (2009 (1976)). *Western Attitudes Toward Death: From the Middle Ages to the Present*. London: Marion Boyars.

Aristotle (1976). *Nichomachean Ethics*. London: Penguin.

Arnold, M.B. (1960). *Emotion and Personality*. New York: Columbia University Press.

Arnott, P.D. (1991). *Public and Performance in the Greek Theatre*. London: Taylor & Francis.

Attig, T. (2004). Meanings of death seen through the lens of grieving. *Death Studies*, 28, 341–60.

Attig, T. (2011). *How We Grieve: Relearning the World*. 2nd edn. Oxford: Oxford University Press.

Ayer, A.J. (1990 (1936)). *Language, Truth and Logic*. London: Penguin.

Bandini, J. (2015). The medicalization of bereavement:

(Ab)normal grief in the DSM-5. *Death Studies*, 39, 347–52.

Barber, B. (2007). *Consumed: How Markets Corrupt Children, Infantilize Adults, and Swallow Citizens Whole*. New York: W.W. Norton & Co.

Beck, U. (2001). Living your own life in a runaway world: Individualisation, globalisation and politics. In W. Hutton and A. Giddens (eds.), *On the Edge: Living with Global Capitalism*. London: Vintage.

Becker, E. (2011 (1973)). *The Denial of Death*. London: Souvenir Press.

Bennett, M.R. and Hacker, P.M.S. (2003). *Philosophical Foundations of Neuroscience*. Oxford: Blackwell.

Bolton, D. (2008). *What is Mental Disorder? An Essay in Philosophy, Science, and Values*. Oxford: Oxford University Press.

Boorse, C. (1976). What a theory of mental health should be. *Journal for the Theory of Social Behaviour*, 6, 61–84.

Bowker, G.C. and Star, S.L. (2000). *Sorting Things Out: Classification and Its Consequences*. Cambridge, MA: The MIT Press.

Brescó, I. and Wagoner, B. (not yet published). Memory, mourning and memorials.

Brinkmann, S. (2006a). Damasio on mind and emotions: A conceptual critique. *Nordic Psychology*, 58, 366–80.

Brinkmann, S. (2006b). Mental life in the space of reasons. *Journal for the Theory of Social Behaviour*, 36, 1–16.

Brinkmann, S. (2009). *Psyken – mellem synapser og samfund*. Aarhus: Aarhus Universitetsforlag.

Brinkmann, S. (2011). Towards an expansive hybrid psychology: Integrating theories of the mediated mind. *Integrative Psychological and Behavioral Science*, 45, 1–20.

Brinkmann, S. (2014a). Psychiatric diagnoses as semiotic mediators: The case of ADHD. *Nordic Psychology*, 66, 121–34.

Brinkmann, S. (2014b). *Stå fast – et opgør med tidens udviklingstvang*. Copenhagen: Gyldendal.

Brinkmann, S. (2016a). *Diagnostic Cultures: A Cultural Approach to the Pathologization of Modern Life*. London: Routledge.

Brinkmann, S. (2016b). Psychology as a normative science. In J. Valsiner, G. Marsico, N. Chaudhary, T. Sato and V. Dazzani (eds.), *Psychology as the Science of Human Being: The Yokohama Manifesto*. New York: Springer, pp. 3–16.

Brinkmann, S. (2016c). *Ståsteder: 10 gamle ideer til en ny verden*. Copenhagen: Gyldendal.

Brinkmann, S. (2017a). *Persons and their Minds: Towards an Integrative Theory of the Mediated Mind*. London: Routledge.

Brinkmann, S. (2017b). Perspectives on diagnosed suffering. *Nordic Psychology*, 69, 1–4.

Brinkmann, S. and Kofod, E.H. (2018). Grief as an extended emotion. *Culture & Psychology*, 24(2), 160–73.

Brinkmann, S. and Kvale, S. (2015). *InterViews: Learning the Craft of Qualitative Research Interviewing*. 3rd edn. Thousand Oaks, CA: Sage.

Brinkmann, S. and Musaeus, P. (2012). Emotions and the moral order. *Lodz: Studies in Language*, 27, 123–37.

Bibliography

Brinkmann, S. and Petersen, A. (2015). *Diagnoser: Perspektiver, kritik og diskussion.* Aarhus: Klim.

Brinkmann, S., Brescó, I., Kofod, E.H., Køster, A., Overvad, A.T., Petersen, A., Suhr, A., Tateo, L., Wagoner, B. and Winther-Lindqvist, D. (not yet published). The presence of grief: Research-based art and arts-based research on grief. *Qualitative Inquiry.*

Butler, J. (2005). *Giving an Account of Oneself.* New York: Fordham University Press.

Clark, A. (2008). *Supersizing the Mind: Embodiment, Action and Cognitive Extension.* Cambridge: Cambridge University Press.

Clark, A. and Chalmers, D. (1998). The extended mind. *Analysis,* 58, 7–19.

Cockburn, D. (2009). Emotion, expression and conversation. In Y. Gustafsson, C. Kronqvist and M. McEachrane (eds.), *Emotions and Understanding: Wittgensteinian Perspectives.* Basingstoke: Palgrave Macmillan, pp. 126–44.

Colombetti, G. and Krueger, J. (2015). Scaffoldings of the affective mind. *Philosophical Psychology,* 28, 1157–76.

Conrad, P. (2007). *The Medicalization of Society.* Baltimore: The Johns Hopkins University Press.

Cosmides, L. and Tooby, J. (1997). 'Evolutionary Psychology: A Primer', at http://www.cep.ucsb.edu/primer.html.

Crisafi, A. and Gallagher, S. (2010). Hegel and the extended mind. *AI & Society,* 25, 123–29.

Critchley, S. (2010). *How to Stop Living and Start Worrying: Conversations with Carl Cederström.* Cambridge: Polity Press.

Crowell, S. (2009). Husserlian phenomenology. In

Bibliography

H. Dreyfus and M. Wrathall (eds.), *A Companion to Phenomenology and Existentialism*. Oxford: Wiley-Blackwell, pp. 9–30.

Damasio, A. (1994). *Descartes' Error: Emotion, Reason, and the Human Brain*. New York: Quill.

Damasio, A. (1999). *The Feeling of What Happens: Body, Emotion and the Making of Consciousness*. London: Vintage.

Davies, W. (2015). *The Happiness Industry: How the Government and Big Business Sold Us Well-Being*. London: Verso.

Davis, C. (1996). *Levinas: An Introduction*. Cambridge: Polity.

Descartes, R. (2017). *Meditations on First Philosophy*. 2nd edn. Cambridge: Cambridge University Press.

Didion, J. (2005). *The Year of Magical Thinking*. London: Fourth Estate.

Doka, K.J. (2016). *Grief is a Journey: Finding Your Path Through Loss*. New York: Atria Books.

Draghi-Lorenz, R., Reddy, V. and Costall, A. (2001). Rethinking the development of 'nonbasic' emotions: A critical review of existing theories. *Developmental Review*, 21, 263–304.

DuBose, T. (1997). The phenomenology of bereavement, grief, and mourning. *Journal of Religion and Health*, 36, 367–74.

Ekman, P. (1992). An argument for basic emotions. *Cognition and Emotion*, 6, 169–200.

Freud, S. (1990). *Inhibitions, Symptoms and Anxiety*. New York: W.W. Norton & Co.

Freud, S. (2005). *On Murder, Mourning and Melancholia*. London: Penguin Classics.

Fuchs, T. (2018). Presence in absence: The ambiguous

phenomenology of grief. *Phenomenology and the Cognitive Sciences*, 17, 43–63.

Gaita, R. (2005). *The Philosopher's Dog: Friendships with Animals*. London: Random House.

Gallagher, S. (2013). The socially extended mind. *Cognitive Systems Research*, 25–6, 4–12.

Geertz, C. (1983). *Local Knowledge: Further Essays in Interpretive Anthropology*. New York: Basic Books.

Gerrod Parrott, W. and Harré, R. (2001). Princess Diana and the emotionology of contemporary Britain. *International Journal of Group Tensions*, 30, 29–38.

Gier, N.F. (1981). *Wittgenstein and Phenomenology: A Comparative Study of the Later Wittgenstein, Husserl, Heidegger and Merleau-Ponty*. Albany, NY: State University of New York Press.

Giorgi, A. (1975). An application of phenomenological method in psychology. In A. Giorgi, C. Fischer and E. Murray (eds.), *Duquesne Studies in Phenomenological Psychology II*. Pittsburgh, PA: Duquesne University Press.

Gjedde, A. (2015). Sygdomme har ingen kendt årsag. *Politiken*, 13 September, 12.

Glaser, B.G. and Strauss, A. (1967). *The Discovery of Grounded Theory: Strategies for Qualitative Research*. New York: Aldine Publishing Company.

Granek, L. (2010). Grief as pathology: The evolution of grief theory in psychology from Freud to the present. *History of Psychology*, 13, 46–73.

Granek, L. (2013). Disciplinary wounds: Has grief become the identified patient for a field gone awry? *Journal of Loss and Trauma*, 18, 275–88.

Griffiths, P. and Scarantino, A. (2009). Emotions in the wild: The situated perspective on emotion. In

M. Aydede and P. Robbins (eds.), *The Cambridge Handbook of Situated Cognition*. Cambridge: Cambridge University Press, pp. 437–53.

Gross, R. (2016). *Understanding Grief*. London: Routledge.

Guðmundsdóttir, M. (2009). Embodied grief: Bereaved parents' narratives of their suffering body. *OMEGA: Journal of Death and Dying*, 59, 253–69.

Guldin, M. (2014). *Tab og sorg: En grundbog for professionelle*. Copenhagen: Hans Reitzels Forlag.

Gumbrecht, H.U. (2004). *Production of Presence: What Meaning Cannot Convey*. Stanford, CA: Stanford University Press.

Hallam, E. and Hockey, J. (2001). *Death, Memory and Material Culture*. Oxford: Berg.

Harré, R. (1983). *Personal Being*. Oxford: Basil Blackwell.

Harré, R. (2009). Emotions as cognitive-affective-somatic hybrids. *Emotion Review*, 1, 294–301.

Haslam, N.O. (2014). Natural kinds in psychiatry: Conceptually implausible, empirically questionable, and stigmatizing. In H. Kincaid and J. Sullivan (eds.), *Classifying Psychopathology: Mental Kinds and Natural Kinds*. Cambridge, MA: The MIT Press.

Heidegger, M. (1962 (1927)). *Being and Time*. New York: HarperCollins Publishers.

Helm, B. (2009). Emotions as evaluative feelings. *Emotion Review*, 1, 248–55.

Hochschild, A.R. (1979). Emotion work, feeling rules, and social structure. *American Journal of Sociology*, 85, 551–75.

Horwitz, A.V. and Wakefield, J.C. (2005). The Age of Depression. *The Public Interest*, 158, 39–58.

Bibliography

Horwitz, A.V. and Wakefield, J.C. (2007). *The Loss of Sadness: How Psychiatry Transformed Normal Sorrow into Depressive Disorder*. Oxford: Oxford University Press.

Jacobsen, M.H. (2016). 'Spectacular death': Proposing a new fifth phase to Philippe Ariès's admirable history of death. *Humanities*, 5, 1–20.

Jacobsen, M.H. and Kofod, E.H. (2015). Sorg – en fraværsfølelse under forandringq. In I. G. Bo and M.H. Jacobsen (eds.), *Hverdagslivets følelser*. Copenhagen: Hans Reitzels Forlag, pp. 245–79.

James, W. (1983 (1890)). *The Principles of Psychology*. Cambridge, MA: Harvard University Press.

Jaspers, K. (1997 (1959)). *General Psychopathology*. Baltimore, MA: The Johns Hopkins University Press.

Johnson, M. (2007). *The Meaning of the Body: Aesthetics of Human Understanding*. Chicago: University of Chicago Press.

Jordan, A.H. and Litz, B.T. (2014). Prolonged grief disorder: Diagnostic, assessment, and treatment considerations. *Professional Psychology: Research and Practice*, 45, 180–7.

Kant, I. (1998 (1781)). *Critique of Pure Reason*. Cambridge: Cambridge University Press.

Karlsson, G. and Sjöberg, L. (2009). The experiences of guilt and shame: A phenomenological-psychological study. *Human Studies*, 32, 335–55.

Katz, J. (1996). The social psychology of Adam and Eve. *Theory & Society*, 25, 545–82.

Katz, J. (1999). *How Emotions Work*. Chicago: University of Chicago Press.

Kerrigan, M. (2007). *The History of Death: Burial*

Customs and Funeral Rites, from the Ancient World to Modern Times. London: The Lyons Press.

Kierkegaard, S. (1954) *Fear and Trembling* and *The Sickness Unto Death.* Princeton: Princeton University Press.

Kierkegaard, S. (1980). *The Concept of Anxiety.* Princeton: Princeton University Press.

Klass, D., Silverman, P.R. and Nickman, S.L. (1996). *Continuing Bonds: New Understandings of Grief.* New York: Routledge.

Kofod, E.H. (2015). Grief as a border diagnosis. *Ethical Human Psychology and Psychiatry*, 17, 109–24.

Kofod, E.H. (2017). From morality to pathology: A brief historization of contemporary Western grief practices and understandings. *Nordic Psychology*, 69, 47–60.

Kofod, E.H. and Brinkmann, S. (2017). Grief as a normative phenomenon: The diffuse and ambivalent normativity of infant loss and parental grieving in contemporary Western culture. *Culture & Psychology*, 23(4), 519–33.

Köhler, W. (1959 (1938)). *The Place of Value in a World of Facts.* New York: Meridian Books.

Krueger, J. (2014). Varieties of extended emotions. *Phenomenology and the Cognitive Sciences*, 13, 533–55.

Kuhn, T.S. (1970). *The Structure of Scientific Revolutions.* 2nd edn. Chicago: University of Chicago Press.

Lane, C. (2007). *Shyness: How Normal Behavior Became a Sickness.* New Haven: Yale University Press.

Lazarus, R. (1991). *Emotion and Adaptation.* Oxford: Oxford University Press.

Lear, J. (2006). *Radical Hope: Ethics in the Face of*

193

Cultural Devastation. Cambridge, MA: Harvard University Press.

Lesch, W. (2001). Cultivating emotions: Some ethical perspectives. *Ethical Theory and Moral Practice*, 4, 105–8.

Levinas, E. (1969). *Totality and Infinity: An Essay on Exteriority*. Pittsburgh: Duquesne University Press.

Lewis, C.S. (1961). *A Grief Observed*. London: Faber and Faber.

MacIntyre, A. (1999). *Dependent Rational Animals: Why Human Beings Need the Virtues*. London: Duckworth.

McGann, P.J. (2011). Troubling diagnoses. In P.J. McGann and D.J. Hutson (eds.), *Sociology of Diagnosis*. Bingley: Emerald, pp. 331–62.

McLennan, G. (2010). The postsecular turn. *Theory, Culture & Society*, 27, 3–20.

Madsen, O.J. and Brinkmann, S. (2012). Lost in paradise: *Paradise Hotel* and the showcase of shamelessness. *Cultural Studies – Critical Methodologies*, 12, 459–67.

Mammen, J. (1996). *Den menneskelige sans: Et essay om psykologiens genstandsområde*. 3rd end. Copenhagen: Dansk Psykologisk Forlag.

Mammen, J. and Mironenko, I. (2015). Activity theories and the ontology of psychology: Learning from Danish and Russian experiences. *Integrative Psychological and Behavioral Science*, 49, 681–713.

Mead, G.H. (2015 (1934)). *Mind, Self, and Society*. Chicago: University of Chicago Press.

Merleau-Ponty, M. (2012 (1945)). *Phenomenology of Perception*. London: Routledge.

Mol, A. (2008). I eat an apple: On theorizing subjectivity. *Subjectivity*, 22, 28–37.

Mongelluzzo, N.B. (2013). *Understanding Loss and Grief: A Guide Through Life Changing Events*. Lanham, MD: Rowman & Littlefield.

Moors, A., Ellsworth, P.C., Scherer, K.R. and Frijda, N.H. (2013). Appraisal theories of emotion: State of the art and future development. *Emotion Review*, 5, 119–24.

Nussbaum, M.C. (1986). *The Fragility of Goodness: Luck and Ethics in Greek Tragedy and Philosophy*. Cambridge: Cambridge University Press.

Nussbaum, M.C. (2001). *Upheavals of Thought: The Intelligence of Emotions*. Cambridge: Cambridge University Press.

O'Connor, M.-F. (2013). Physiological mechanisms and the neurobiology of complicated grief. In M. Stroebe, H. Schut and J. van den Bout (eds.), *Complicated Grief: Scientific Foundations for Health Care Professionals*. London: Routledge, pp. 204–18.

Papadatou, D. (2015). Childhood death and bereavement across cultures. In C.M. Parkes, P. Laungani and B. Young (eds.), *Death and Bereavement Across Cultures*. 2nd edn. London: Routledge, pp. 151–65.

Parkes, C.M. (1972). *Bereavement: Studies of Grief in Adult Life*. London: Tavistock.

Parkes, C.M. (1998). Traditional models and theories of grief. *Bereavement Care*, 17, 21–3.

Parkes, C.M. (2014). Diagnostic criteria for complications of bereavement in the DSM-5. *Bereavement Care*, 33, 113–17.

Parkes, C.M. and Prigerson, H. (2010). *Bereavement:*

Studies of Grief in Adult Life. 4th edn. London: Penguin.

Parkes, C.M., Laungani, P. and Young, B. (2015). Introduction. In C.M. Parkes, P. Laungani and B. Young (eds.), *Death and Bereavement Across Cultures*. 2nd edn. London: Routledge, pp. 3–8.

Pelias, R. (2004). *A Methodology of the Heart: Evoking Academic and Daily Life*. Walnut Creek, CA: AltaMira Press.

Piper, W.E. and Ogrodniczuk, J. (2013). Brief group therapies for complicated grief. In M. Stroebe, H. Schut and J. van den Bout (eds.), *Complicated Grief: Scientific Foundations for Health Care Professionals*. London: Routledge, pp. 263–77.

Prigerson, H.G. and Maciejweski, P.K. (2006). A call for sound empirical testing and evaluation of criteria for complicated grief proposed for DSM-V. *OMEGA: Journal of Death and Dying*, 52, 9–19.

Prigerson, H. et al. (2009). Prolonged grief disorder: Psychometric validation of criteria proposed for DSM-V and ICD-11. *PLOS Medicine*, 6, 1–12.

Putnam, H. (1975). The meaning of 'meaning'. In *Mind, Language and Reality: Philosophical Papers, Volume 2*. Cambridge: Cambridge University Press.

Ratcliffe, M. (2017). The phenomenological clarification of grief and its relevance for psychiatry. In G. Stanghellini, M. Broome, A.V. Fernandez, P. Fusar-Poli, A. Raballo and R. Rosfort (eds.), *The Oxford Handbook of Phenomenological Psychopathology*. Oxford: Oxford University Press, pp. 1–19.

Rosenberg, C.E. (2007). *Our Present Complaint: American Medicine, Then and Now*. Baltimore: The Johns Hopkins University Press.

Rosenblatt, P.C. (2001). A social constructivist perspective on cultural differences in grief. In M. Stroebe, R. Hasson, W. Stroebe and H. Schut (eds.), *Handbook of Bereavement Research: Consequences, Coping, and Care*. Washington, DC: American Psychological Association, pp. 285–300.

Sartre, J.-P. (2006 (1939)). *Sketch for a Theory of the Emotions*. Abingdon: Routledge.

Schacter, D. and Singer, J. (1962). Cognitive, social, and psychological determinants of emotional states. *Psychological Review*, 69, 379–99.

Scheer, M. (2012). Are emotions a kind of practice (and is that what makes them have a history)? A Bourdieuian approach to understanding emotions. *History and Theory*, 51, 193–220.

Scheff, T.J. (2003). Shame in self and society. *Symbolic Interaction*, 26, 239–62.

Scheper-Hughes, N. (1993). *Death Without Weeping: The Violence of Everyday Life in Brazil*. Berkeley: University of California Press.

Seale, C. (1998). *Constructing Death: The Sociology of Dying and Bereavement*. Cambridge: Cambridge University Press.

Serres, M. (2015 (1987)). *Statues: The Second Book of Foundations*. London: Bloomsbury.

Shear, K., Reynolds, C.F., Simon, N.M., Zisook, S., Wang, Y. and Mauro, C. et al. (2016). Optimizing treatment of complicated grief: A randomized clinical trial. *JAMA Psychiatry*, 73, 685–94.

Shweder, R.A. (2008). The cultural psychology of suffering: The many meanings of health in Orissa, India (and elsewhere). *Ethos*, 36, 60–77.

Slaby, J. (2014). Emotions and the extended mind.

In C. von Scheve and M. Salmela (eds.), *Collective Emotions*. Oxford: Oxford University Press, pp. 32–46.

Solomon, R.C. (2007). *True to Our Feelings: What Our Emotions Are Really Telling Us*. Oxford: Oxford University Press.

Stearns, P.N. and Knapp, M. (1996). Historical perspectives on grief. In R. Harré and W. Gerrod Parrott (eds.), *The Emotions: Social, Cultural and Biological Dimensions*. Thousand Oaks: Sage, pp. 132–50.

Sterelny, K. (2012). *The Evolved Apprentice: How Evolution Made Humans Unique*. Cambridge, MA: The MIT Press.

Taylor, C. (1989). *Sources of the Self*. Cambridge: Cambridge University Press.

Trevarthen, C. (1993). The self born in intersubjectivity: The psychology of an infant communicating. In U. Neisser (ed.), *The Perceived Self*. Cambridge: Cambridge University Press.

Valsiner, J., Marsico, G., Chaudhary, N., Sato, T. and Dazzani, V. (2016). *Psychology as the Science of Human Being: The Yokohama Manifesto*. New York: Springer.

Vygotsky, L.S. (1978). *Mind in Society: The Development of Higher Psychological Processes*. Cambridge, MA: Harvard University Press.

Wakefield, J.C. (1992). The concept of mental disorder: On the boundary between biological facts and social values. *American Psychologist*, 47, 373–88.

Wakefield, J.C. (2012). Should prolonged grief be reclassified as a mental disorder in DSM-5? Reconsidering the empirical and conceptual arguments for complicated grief disorder. *Journal of Nervous and Mental Disease*, 200, 499–511.

Wakefield, J.C. (2013a). DSM-5 grief scorecard: Assessment and outcomes of proposals to pathologize grief. *World Psychiatry*, 12, 171–3.

Wakefield, J.C. (2013b). Is complicated/prolonged grief a disorder? Why the proposal to add a category of complicated grief disorder to the DSM-5 is conceptually and empirically unsound. In M. Stroebe, H. Schut and J. van den Bout (eds.), *Complicated Grief: Scientific Foundations for Health Care Professionals.* London: Routledge, pp. 99–114.

Walter, T. (1999). *On Bereavement: The Culture of Grief.* Maidenhead: Open University Press.

Walter, T. (2019). The pervasive dead. *Mortality*, 24, 389–404.

Wetherell, M. (2012). *Affect and Emotion: A New Social Science Understanding.* London: Sage.

Williams, R.F.G. (2009). Everyday sorrows are not mental disorders: The clash between psychiatry and Western cultural habits. *Prometheus*, 27, 47–70.

Wittgenstein, L. (1958). *Philosophical Investigations.* 2nd edn. Oxford: Basil Blackwell.

Zajonc, R. (1984). On the primacy of affect. *American Psychologist*, 39, 117–23.

Zinck, A. and Newen, A. (2008). Classifying emotion: A developmental account. *Synthese*, 161, 1–25.